DEATH ALGORITHM AND
:R DIGITAL DILEMMAS

UNTIMELY MEDITATIONS

1. *THE AGONY OF EROS*
   Byung-Chul Han

2. *ON HITLER'S* MEIN KAMPF: *THE POETICS OF NATIONAL SOCIALISM*
   Albrecht Koschorke

3. *IN THE SWARM: DIGITAL PROSPECTS*
   Byung-Chul Han

4. *THE TERROR OF EVIDENCE*
   Marcus Steinweg

5. *ALL AND NOTHING: A DIGITAL APOCALYPSE*
   Martin Burckhardt and Dirk Höfer

6. *POSITIVE NIHILISM: MY CONFRONTATION WITH HEIDEGGER*
   Hartmut Lange

7. *INCONSISTENCIES*
   Marcus Steinweg

8. *SHANZHAI: DECONSTRUCTION IN CHINESE*
   Byung-Chul Han

9. *TOPOLOGY OF VIOLENCE*
   Byung-Chul Han

10. *THE RADICAL FOOL OF CAPITALISM: ON JEREMY BENTHAM, THE PANOPTICON, AND THE AUTO-ICON*
    Christian Welzbacher

11. *GERMAN PHILOSOPHY: A DIALOGUE*
    Alain Badiou and Jean-Luc Nancy

12. *PORTRAIT OF THE MANAGER AS A YOUNG AUTHOR: ON STORY-TELLING, BUSINESS, AND LITERATURE*
    Philipp Schönthaler

13. *WASTE: A NEW MEDIA PRIMER*
    Roberto Simanowski

14. *THE DEATH ALGORITHM AND OTHER DIGITAL DILEMMAS*
    Roberto Simanowski

THE MIT PRESS
CAMBRIDGE, MASSACHUSETTS
LONDON, ENGLAND

THE DEATH ALGORITHM AND OTHER DIGITAL DILEMMAS

ROBERTO SIMANOWSKI

TRANSLATED BY JEFFERSON CHASE

This book was set in PF DinText Pro by Toppan Best-set Premedia Limited. Printed and bound in the United States of America.

Library of Congress Cataloging-in-Publication Data

Names: Simanowski, Roberto, author. | Chase, Jefferson S., translator.
Title: The death algorithm and other digital dilemmas / Roberto Simanowski ; translated by Jefferson Chase.
Description: Cambridge, MA : MIT Press, 2018. | Series: Untimely meditations ; 14 | Includes bibliographical references.
Identifiers: LCCN 2018015411 | ISBN 9780262536370 (pbk. : alk. paper)
Subjects: LCSH: Internet—Moral and ethical aspects. | Telecommunication—Philosophy. | Telematics—Moral and ethical aspects. | Digital media—Social aspects.
Classification: LCC TK5105.878 .S55 2018 | DDC 174/.9004—dc23 LC record available at https://lccn.loc.gov/2018015411

10   9   8   7   6   5   4   3   2   1

CONTENTS

INTRODUCTION: COMING PREDICAMENTS   vii

1 BULLSHIT AND FAST FOOD   1
2 SMARTPHONE ZOMBIES   21
3 MARSHMALLOW CULTURE   37
4 TRAFFIC COPS AND MEDIA EDUCATION   49
5 CANNIBALISM AND NEW MEDIA   87
6 UBER-DRIVE   99
7 THE DEATH ALGORITHM   123

NOTES   153

INTRODUCTION: COMING PREDICAMENTS

Lavater

It's strange how the past can catch up with you. I can still picture myself as a student of literature and history sitting in my university library trying to get through Johann Caspar Lavater's *Physiognomic Fragments* from 1775–78. It consisted of multiple volumes in which the author, a pastor from Zurich, used various hand-drawn portraits to argue that you could determine people's characters by examining their facial features. I thought it was a pretty wild thesis. Why should external and biological attributes reflect internal and cultural characteristics? But I was only just starting out in my studies. Perhaps I simply didn't understand the full complexity of the situation. After all, it seemed true that, as Lavater argued, you could always identify the villain on a theatrical stage before he or she had uttered a word.

Thus were my thoughts at the time. I was recently reminded of Lavater by a startup, founded in 2014 in Tel Aviv, which defines its mission as "to understand humans through a single piece of personal information: an image of a face."[1] On the basis of its research in the field of social and life sciences, particularly on twins, "Faception" hopes to be able to recognize at a glance whether an individual is "a potential pedophile, an aggressive person, or a criminal." Unlike Lavater's arguments, the company's logic is, they contend, strictly scientific and combines two central assumptions: that "genetics played a large role in determining face shape" and that "genes play a greater role in determining key personality traits like social skills and learning ability than the way we are brought up by our parents."[2]

Faception's services are aimed primarily at security companies, but their implications go much further. The company proclaims: "Being able to utilize facial images to also answer the questions 'What is this person? What are his personality traits? What motivates him?' could revolutionize how companies, organizations and even robots understand people, and dramatically improve public safety, communications, decision-making, and experiences."[3] The promise of better interaction via artificial intelligence echoes the subtitle of Lavater's monumental work, "On the Promotion of Human Knowledge and Human Love." It was a false promise back then. After all, who wants to get to know people with fierce facial expressions if it's considered scientifically proven that those facial features are not just the pitiable results of unfortunate genetic combinations but the external impressions of an internal state?

The promise that Faception software will improve human interaction could turn into a nightmare once the product is used beyond airports, subway stations, and other enhanced security locations. Algorithmic screening could be used to analyze new members of a health club, job applicants, and potential partners on a dating site before people have a chance to speak for themselves. Ultimately, the only limits on the human drive for knowledge are technological. Anything that can be measured will be measured, in the name of transparency, enlightenment, and truth. Who would think about getting in the way of such a noble cause or the technological innovations that result from it?

How can human beings be persuaded to go along with extremely problematic technological innovations? In his novel *The Circle*, Dave Eggers answers this question when he has his fictional CEO Eamon Bailey argue for the desirability of general surveillance technology using the seemingly harmless example of surfers. Surfers are always asking how the waves are at a given beach and whether they're worth the trip. They can of course call the local surf shop or "buddies who might have gotten out to the beach before," but at some point they stop answering their phones. The solution is a camera concealed in the reeds that surfers can access via the Internet. It goes without saying such technology can be used not only to check out the weather at Stinson or Ocean Beach, but to monitor what's happening in your own backyard at home. The idea of sharing is likewise obvious. "If you have one thousand friends, and they have ten cameras each, you now have ten thousand options for live footage," Eamon says. The fact that such a massive surveillance network can also effectively recognize human rights violations, for example with "protesters on the streets of Egypt," reveals the political aspect of the camera. As its name "SeeChange" makes clear, its use is by no means confined to areas of surf culture. It applies to culture in general. "Transparency leads to peace of mind," Eamon proclaims.

After citing buzzwords like "documentation and accountability" and "Second Enlightenment," the CEO concludes his speech to the team of workers at the Circle Empire by demanding: "All that happens must be known." The company employees, prepared to wage total war against nontransparency and privacy, leap from their seats and repeat that maxim as though in a trance.

Regressive Progress

"Technological progress cannot be allowed to socially regress," German Justice Minister Heiko Maas warned at a 2017 conference on legal and ethical concerns in the digital world entitled "Connected. Measured. Sold?" In the digital world, Maas added, one primary consideration is that "human beings should never be reduced to mere objects of algorithms. The minister called, on the one hand, for a "transparency requirement for algorithms," and, on the other, for a general "right to an analog world."[4] This requirement and this right are clearly not given in the two examples just cited. The technological progress represented by SeeChange and Faception do in fact entail a social step backward, if we consider what the German sociologist Georg Simmel wrote in 1907: "Secrets—the concealment of reality using either positive or negative means—are one of the greatest intellectual achievements of humankind."[5]

Admittedly, citing a long-dead early-twentieth-century German sociologist isn't a particularly effective argument against the technologies that enthusiastic computer geeks and visionary IT entrepreneurs find so cool more than a century later. Using the hollow argument that privacy is a relatively late and above all Western phenomenon in the history of human culture, many observers are already preparing themselves to submit without resistance to a postprivate age.[6] Is it perhaps a mere question of time before, as happens in *The Circle*, politicians more or less voluntarily wear cameras on their lapels in the name of transparency—as a sign of uninterrupted, universal accountability to their voters?

The social advances jeopardized by such "backward progress" include political achievements such as the minimum wage, workers' right to paid vacations, and other social benefits increasingly under threat from platform capitalism and the gig economy. In April 2017, the *New York Times* described the problem: "Uber and the like may be taking the economy back toward a pre–New Deal era when businesses had enormous power over workers and few checks on their ability to exploit it." For that reason, by 2015, German Justice Minister Maas was already calling for a "digital new deal" to impose "democratic rules on big data" and to prevent a "digital day labor system." Politicians have realized that the problems associated with digital society go far beyond just privacy and surveillance.[7]

Nonetheless, the inverse relationship between technological and social progress is by no means a phenomenon of the start of this new digital era. At its inception as a mass-effective medium, the Internet promised structural advantages for small-time entrepreneurs vis-à-vis super-regional market leaders. The beginning was the heyday of secrecy, as Peter Steiner's famous *New Yorker* cartoon from July 1993 perfectly underscored. It featured two canines sitting in front of a computer with the caption: "On the Internet, no one knows you're a dog." Back then, you were what you typed—and only that—on the Internet. Back then, you could conceal not only your face, but your skin color, age, gender, and all external indications of your specific social background. What you were for others depended solely on what you wrote. But then even computing history underwent its "visual turn." A quarter of a century later, it is no longer A that determines what B knows about A. B consults Internet databases for more information on A. And perhaps B will also soon use facial recognition software and camera systems that put every bit of the offline world on the Net, which can be searched easily and precisely for images of A.

Technology Out of Control

Faception touts its product as a technology that "allows predictive screening solutions and enables Preventive Actions."[8] Yet despite all of the talk today about "predictive" and "prescriptive" analytics, no one would claim that we are now better able to foresee the consequences of our actions and, in particular, our inventions. We sense the gloomy truth of this whenever we're confronted with artificial intelligence, and are forced to ask whether the robots that will drive our cars, manage our cities, and organize our lives in future may someday turn against us. The threat posed to humans by their own creations has been a literary trope since Mary Shelley's novel *Frankenstein, or The Modern Prometheus* (1818) and Goethe's lyric poem "The Sorcerer's Apprentice"

(1797), the latter of which features a would-be magician who in the absence of his master can no longer rid himself of the spirits he has summoned. Both texts envision scenarios in which man becomes god and breathes life into other creatures. In so doing, people are to an extent following their historical calling, identified by Kant in 1784, of completely developing and using the gift of reason with which nature has endowed them. But it is very questionable whether Kant, were he alive today, would see the passing of that faculty to artificial intelligence as the triumph or the ultimate failure of reason.[9]

The specialist term at the moment for spirits that threaten to get out of control is "deep learning." Deep learning subjects software to various learning procedures in a black box whose internal operations and functions remain impenetrable to humans. Its logical extension will mean that we will no longer be able to understand, but only accept and reject many decisions taken by algorithms. It's incumbent upon us to ask before innovations are developed: What do we actually know about the consequences of their actions? Can all of the effects ever be foreseen? And the aftereffects of the effects?

In his 1936 essay "The Unanticipated Consequences of Purposive Social Action," American sociologist Robert K. Merton answered these questions in the negative, noting that international actions can have unanticipated and undesired consequences because of human ignorance, miscalculations, or lack of foresight. Even back then, Merton understood that such ignorance resulted from an economically based lack of the desire to learn: "In our present economic order, it is manifestly uneconomical behavior to concern ourselves with attempts to obtain knowledge for predicting the outcomes of action to such an extent that we have practically no time or energy for other pursuits."[10] Even more important than this sort of prioritization is the self-deception entailed by the idea that the immediate consequences are also the desired ones. "Action in accordance with a dominant set of values tends to be focused upon that particular value [sic]," Merton proposes. But he adds: "With the complex interaction which constitutes society, action ramifies. Its consequences are not restricted to the specific area in which they were initially intended to center. They occur in interrelated fields explicitly ignored at that time of action."[11]

Merton, too, invokes Goethe, albeit *Faust* and not the "The Sorcerer's Apprentice." In Goethe's masterpiece, the demon Mephisto famously declares himself to be "part of that power which would / Do evil constantly and constantly does good." Merton reverses this dialectic. An "essential paradox of social action," he writes, is that "the 'realization' of values may lead to their renunciation. We may paraphrase Goethe and speak of 'Die Kraft, die stets das Gute will, und stets das Böse schafft' [that power which would do good constantly, and constantly does evil]."[12]

An illustration of Merton's reversed dialectic is the "like" button, which came into considerable public discredit in late 2017 for allegedly lulling society into an endless loop of dopamine feedback. In its defense, one of the button's inventors, Justin Rosenstein, unconsciously recapitulated Merton's statement when he generalized his own ignorance of the repercussions of his work into a human condition: "It is very common, for humans to develop things with the best of intentions and for them to have unintended, negative consequences."[13]

Perhaps understandably, amid the criticism of the "like" button, no one thought to mention the atom bomb. Yet comparisons between the two are legitimate insofar as nuclear fission was originally developed to promote the welfare of humankind, and the "like" button was invented not to harm people but as a sensible-seeming communication aid. Ten years on from its invention, it's clear that the button serves less to spread "little bits of positivity" than to create "bright dings of pseudo-pleasure" that leave people needing constant fixes of dopamine—a phenomenon brilliantly if terrifyingly depicted in the social-ranking dystopia episode "Nosedive" of the British TV series *Black Mirror*.[14]

The Tragedy of Culture

When Oedipus realized that he had killed his father and slept with his mother, he gouged out his own eyes, punishing himself for something he neither had wanted to do nor even had known he was doing. We can hardly expect similar drastic expressions of regret from Silicon Valley. Those who acknowledge a share of culpability in the division of society by social media have yet to offer up as penance their sight, the hands that wrote the computer code, or at least the fortunes they have earned in the process.

People should be turned away that [?]
[?] their names

Perhaps it is enough for them to acknowledge a measure of guilt since we can equally well question the role of Silicon Valley inventors and entrepreneurs as indispensable agents without whom a historical development would not have been possible. After all, is not the invention of the "like" button and the concomitant mathematization of communication an inherent part of the logic of this technology, of the computer—*nomen est omen*—as an instrument of calculation? Would it have been logical to expect social networks *not* to make use of a function like the "like" button? Was there any real reason to hope that we would subject its potential consequences to empirical analysis before introducing it to the world at large?

In a sense, despite their self-congratulatory self-image as "disruptive innovators," the startups and computer programmers of Silicon Valley are nothing more than the midwives of a technology that wants to be discovered or found—or, to speak with Heidegger, to be "revealed." Things that want to be revealed are at some point simply in the air. No one can prevent them from emerging. One can only refuse to be part of the process—which admittedly would run completely contrary to the self-understanding of inventors and entrepreneurs.[15]

Viewed as part of the philosophy of history, this is a familiar dilemma. Human beings are condemned to subordinate the world, increasingly restricting their own scope of action as they do. Self-alienation is the dialectic opposite of the subjugation of nature. The German philosopher of technology Ernst Cassirer thus asked: "Does not this increased accessibility to the world of objects at the same time necessarily result in the alienation of human beings from their own essence, from what they originally are and what they originally feel?" He identifies "the tragedy of modern culture" in the fact that "all creative cultures increasingly set out certain orders of things for themselves that confront the world of the I in their objective existence and in their being-such-and-such."[16]

Cassirer's moderately pessimistic view of culture and civilization harkens back to German sociologist Georg Simmel's influential essay "The Concept and Tragedy of Culture" (1911). In it, proceeding from a "cultural logic of objects" and an "internal drive of all 'technology,'" Simmel derives an intrinsic logic in all products of the human imagination, which future generations will find very difficult to escape. Seventy years later, German philosopher of technology Hans Jonas would add to this perspective the insight that the human being, unable to escape the logic and need to invent and seduced by his own success, would become "the compulsive executor of his capacity."[17]

If we combine Simmel and Cassirer with Merton and Jonas, we could say that in their obsessive, creative conquest of the world, human beings have also created unforeseen empiric constraints that restrict their freedom for future actions and demand a change of course. Human beings become the victims of their own success. The subject–object dialectic of human activity leads Cassirer to speculate that technology is both the "creation" and the "second creator" of humanity—akin to the famous apocryphal dictum later attributed to Marshall McLuhan: "We shape our tools and thereafter our tools shape us."

It is perhaps not surprising, then, that both Cassirer and Jonas argue respectively for an "ethicization of technology" and an "ethics of the future" that would submit the self-contained nature of technology, which experts and scientists generally accept without question, to a discourse of social control.[18] Insofar as the effects of the digital revolution are already being felt today, we need to think both more for the long term and more profoundly. We need to accept responsibility for analyzing the concealed consequences of every invention that is being pushed forward. Those consequences—which are by no means always as obvious as those of Faception or SeeChange, though often quite foreseeable—need to be taken into consideration when technologies are used practically. Tellingly, Jonas calls the method he advocates to institute the ethics of the future the "heuristics of fear."[19]

In Praise of Dystopia

Whether it's aliens, a meteorite, a new Ice Age, a nuclear war, or genetically manipulated monsters that have escaped from a lab, people have been bombarded for decades now with every imaginable apocalyptic scenario. Dystopias sell as well as sex and crime do. And the disaster films of the future will center around artificial intelligence run amok, a prospect that summons up old fears. Still, the aesthetic formula is not only that of actions movies like Alex Proyas's *I, Robot* (2004), in which rebellious computers wage a war of destruction against humankind. The dangers inherent in this technology are equally imminent in a human-meets-AI love story like Alex Garland's *Ex Machina* (2014). Its ending is more gruesome than that of *I, Robot*, which concludes positively, insofar as the deceived human being will almost certainly die of starvation while the robot will escape undetected into the world at large.

In addition to disobedient robots, the stars of the horror films of the future will be self-driving cars that get hacked by criminals or terrorists, and the Internet of things that will leave society vulnerable and open to blackmail in numerous ways. Villains don't need to hack a nuclear power plant to pose a serious threat. Merely disrupting the power supply is dangerous enough: security experts estimate that it would lead to civil war within three days. The hacking of the power grid in Ukraine, which left around seven hundred thousand households without electricity for hours on December 23, 2015, serves to remind us of how real this threat is.

For hackers, it's child's play to attack the computer systems that regulate our power supply or other crucial control systems of our increasingly networked lives. Governments refuse or perhaps are simply too incompetent to understand: having failed to learn the necessary lessons from being hacked in 2015, Germany again made headlines in early 2018 after discovering its governmental ministries were infected by malware. That hardly encourages us to dismiss gloom-and-doom scenarios as mere alarmism. No matter what threats the disaster films of the future choose, you can bet that somewhere near the start of the picture a disillusioned security expert will inform an overworked politician that there are only two types of companies: those that have gotten hacked and those that don't even know yet that they've gotten hacked.

It's beside the point whether, in taking current security risks to their logical conclusion, disaster movies past and future are trying to warn people to change their ways or simply exploiting the audience's fears. When intellectuals adopt dystopia scenarios in what is often called "cultural criticism" or "cultural pessimism," we can assume that they are trying to highlight and ward off problematic developments by getting people to discuss them. "The prophecy of a coming disaster is done in order to prevent its arrival" is how Jonas once justified the assumption of the worst-case scenario.[20] Dystopias do not represent a pessimistic genre per se. They can also be calls to action. Dystopian authors don't want to be right; they want to be heard. They are forever criticizing current developments in the hope of disrupting what seems to be the preordained course of events. The only people who stop complaining are those who have lost all hope.

The question is, of course, what is seen as problematic not only in Merton's sense of considered action containing unseen chains of casualty, but also in terms of the tolerance society maintains toward certain risks. Both change over time, as illustrated by the examples of asbestos and tobacco, whose health risks first went unrecognized and then were downplayed for a long time. A further question is how society reacts to recognized risks: with prevention, as is the case with the atomic bomb, or with insurance, as is the case with traffic accidents. Here, too, society's attitudes evolve, as should be clear to anyone who lived through the laughable defense drills in both the East and the West in case of a nuclear attack during the Cold War.[21]

As far as the risks associated with digitalization are concerned, society seems satisfied with the insurance model—and not only for individual computer crashes or thefts of data. Even when sensitive infrastructure such as power grids are at risk, foolishness and greed ensure that prevention is rarely pursued comprehensively. Politics and economics both suffer from a "short-termism" that precludes the forward-looking responsibility needed to take credible precautions against possible risks. Part of the reason is that consumer culture and neoliberal finance capitalism have created a "society of carelessness."[22] Another factor is that society, as was not the case with the threat of nuclear war, has little awareness of the risks that its own digitalization entails, not least because of digital technology's seductive promises and already manifest triumphs. We need think only of the convenience of GPS, the accessibility of almost all information at all times and places, the potential reduction of traffic accidents through self-driving cars, and the fight against illness using big data analysis.

A further cause of our carelessness is the lack of victims. Incidents like someone dying in an accident involving a self-driving car or several millions users' data being hacked may briefly raise our awareness of the risk of digitalization. On the whole, though, people are too guided by other experiences (the daily benefits of new technologies) and other worries (terrorism, immigration, populism) to expect their politicians to take up the cause of questioning the digital revolution. Precisely this is the great mistake of our age. People are so focused, for example, on how masses of refugees disrupt the social equilibrium of nation-states that they can easily overlook the enormous changes that the *silent* digital revolution is having on individual and social life. Day by day, piece by piece, dramatic changes are happening all the time without generating any headlines.[23]

The mistake is thinking that something like Faception won't be a success. The mistake is assuming that a surveillance platform like SeeChange can only happen in fiction. The mistake is being convinced that the sort of social scoring system China wants to institute by 2020 and the facial recognition glasses some of its police officers are already wearing is inconceivable in Western democracies. If we take the writing of Simmel, Cassirer, and others about the internal logic of man-made objects and technologies seriously, we need to ask ourselves whether there are any limits to technologies of social control. The sine qua non for such a dangerous development, the digitalization of society and datafication of the individual, are proceeding full-steam ahead. Are not automobile- or health-insurance rewards for people who voluntarily track themselves, demands by employers for full transparency among their employees, and the creation of a culture of ranking by platform-capitalist companies like Uber and Airbnb the first signs that the future of the West will look a lot like China?

Things are already taking their course, and if we let them, they will silently and constantly develop in directions we may not want and may not have even considered possible. Even if technologies like Faception or the "like" button can no longer be avoided, we need to ask how their effects on society might be regulated. The ethicization of technology begins with the public in the domain of culture, where values and visions of civilization are negotiated, and aims at legal regulation as an institutional guarantee of our normative preferences. Only laws, and not mere statements of will, can ensure people's "right to an analog world"—laws that protect those who refuse to go digital and provide an exploitable trail of data from outrageous impositions and disadvantages like high insurance premiums or lesser career chances. We need to discuss the problems of the culture of transparency much more frankly, if we don't want to end up with Chinese-style social scoring. *Principiis obsta*—resist the beginnings—and what better place to start here, too, than with words?

Danger and Salvation

In February 2018, there were news headlines about a group of former Facebook and Google employees forming the Center for Humane Technology to warn people about the negative consequences of social networks and mobile media. Using the slogan "The Truth about Tech" and with seven million dollars in their pockets, the center's founders said they were planning an educational campaign at schools and in the mass media to teach people about the dangers of social media, including the risk of depression that extensive use of such platforms entails. One of the first tasks was to draw up a "ledger of harms" for rank-and-file engineers with "data on the health effects of different technologies and ways to make products that are healthier."[24]

In advance of this news, former Facebook managers launched sharply worded attacks against the platform and distanced themselves from their old jobs.[25] Ironically, the people who got rich off Facebook were now criticizing the source of those riches. Following Pierre Bourdieu, we could speak of an illegitimate conflation of different types of capital. Having acquired economic capital, the ex-managers were now trying to earn social capital. On the other hand, there was little new about this situation. Entrepreneurs have perennially tried to justify their wealth morally with philanthropic activities—Marc Zuckerberg is a perfect example. The difference with the whistleblowers is that they revealed the way in which they acquired their economic capital and thus exposed themselves to criticism, which gave them a measure of credibility.

No matter how one judges this phenomenon, it represents salvation from danger in both senses of the word "from." The "Truth about Tech" campaign reveals and thus protects against a danger, and at the same time, representatives of the danger itself show up to the rescue. German observers might well have felt reminded of Heidegger's famous interpretation of a famous verse by Hölderlin: "But where danger is, grows / The saving power also." Danger, Heidegger proposes, becomes salvation when it is recognized as such. But when the danger is technology itself, it can only be recognized "through our catching sight of what comes to presence in technology, instead of merely staring at the technological," imagining it to be an "instrument" that can be mastered.[26]

Seen through the lens of media studies, Heidegger was pleading for a *strong* concept of media in which they are not simply tools whose concrete instructions for use depend on human decisions but rather essences unto themselves that determine their own uses. McLuhan would later write that "Any medium has the power of imposing its own assumption on the unwary," adding, in his most famous formulation, that "the medium is the message." Salvation from technology begins with recognizing its message and essence. Critical media theorists can only welcome people who helped bring such technologies into existence teaching the public about them—even if those people appropriate social capital in the process. It makes a difference whether it's an academic without a Facebook account or ex–Facebook president Sean Parker warning that "God only knows what it's doing to our children's brains."

Nonetheless, we need to take care that rescuers don't ruin the rescue through sloppiness. Academics have to assist technology experts in their attempts to reveal the essence of technology because that's the academics' great strength, while the technology experts' is far more uncovering technology itself. A good example of this is, again, the "like" button, which was at the center of the former Facebook managers' criticism. While it may be true that the button leads to "short-term dopamine driven feedback loops" that "are ripping apart the social fabric of how society works," it remains unclear why the technology experts conclude that there will be "no civil discourse, no cooperation, misinformation, mistruth."[27] Because people only want to be liked, to the exclusion of everything else? Because people now only post opportunistic pictures? Dopamine jolts notwithstanding, the reason for people's behavior resides in the change wrought by such a feature to human interaction: in the dualism of like/don't like, the lack of reasoning behind value judgments and the mathematicization of evaluation. The more profound danger of the "like" button is that it prevents nuanced positions and decouples evaluation from verbal justification. These are ultimately ideal conditions for populism and fake news, and it is only when our analysis progresses to this causal level that it can come up with suitable responses.

But this doesn't exhaust the problem of the "like" button. On the contrary, this tool leads not just to fake news and "mistruth," but also to a kind of psychometric truth. If we know 150 "likes" a person has handed out, we know more about that person than his or her parents. When that figure reaches 300, we know more than his or her partner, and by 1,000 probably more than that person him- or herself. The "like" button is the epitome of a new form of measuring society, which we need to recognize as a danger of digital technology and its increasingly complete datafication of social and individual behavior. But we have trouble acknowledging this, as became clear in the spring of 2018 when news broke that the British company Cambridge Analytica had gotten hold under questionable circumstances of 50 million Facebook users' data and employed these data to help Trump's campaign send out personally tailored messages in the 2016 US presidential campaign. The most frequently asked questions were: Had Cambridge Analytica done anything illegal? And would the #deletefacebook campaign spell the end of the social media platform? There was little discussion of "dark posts"—the Facebook function allowing the campaign to personalize messages, without which the huge cache of data would have been useless. Even less attention was paid to the "like" button, that function for getting people to continually and unwittingly provide information about themselves, which allows for much more effective and exact forms of manipulation than Cambridge Analytica was ever accused of.

Did commentators avoid these topics because they were afraid of making the discussion too technical? Or because they were too political? Anyone who tried to get beyond the simple story of two evil companies and 87 million victims would have seen the scrupulous data analysis company and the no less rapacious data collection network as symptoms of a new economic and technological order big data is instituting everywhere. The fact that the dark post function had been created for the special needs of Facebook's customers and that the US government does business with Cambridge Analytica's parent company, the Strategic Communication Laboratories Group, should have dissuaded us from understanding the scandal in terms of potentially criminal economic and political acts. On the contrary, the Cambridge Analytica/Facebook revelations raise entirely different questions. Is the much-criticized measuring of psychological traits anything more than the methodological extension of what society has long been doing in the name of social, cognitive, and behavioral science? Is not the use of insights gleaned from such analysis for commercial (personalized advertisements), governmental (nudging), and military (human terrain teams) purposes nothing more than an unavoidable extension of what was already being done? Did we really have any reason to expect that the battle to win the hearts and minds of customers and voters would be waged without the deployment of the latest scientific discoveries and technological possibilities?

These questions allow us to glimpse the real problem at the core of the scandal, beyond the catchy but misleading buzzwords of attack ("data breach," "crime," "misuses") and defense ("bad actors," "breach of trust"). The deeper problem is the essence and the message of technology. The more our social lives can be measured, the less we can deny the knowledge produced or remove ourselves from its practical usage. With digital technologies and social networks, we have created possibilities for measurement and analysis that now ensnare us in their own logic. This is true of the promise that comprehensive knowledge of individual behavior makes for optimizing social processes, for instance, the promises of bettering city planning, energy management by analyzing patterns of energy use, traffic routing by examining people's use of space, and health care by using data on individual nutrition and exercise to diagnose illnesses and initiate preventative measures, if people lead unhealthy lives. Moreover, the trend toward exposing ourselves in the name of social responsibility is supported by our indifference to dangers and our curiosity about what's new. Who really gets that upset that the rating industry (Uber, Airbnb) is harvesting our data? Who opposes the Internet of things just because our refrigerators and electricity meters, and everyone who gains access to them, have a record of our everyday routines? Who loses a minute's sleep over the development of eye-controlled interfaces and technologies for sentiment analyses that promise to anticipate our every want at the same time as they gaze upon our internal thoughts and desires?

Can we really claim to be the victims if companies evaluate our data without our knowledge? Are not all of us, "perpetrators" included, the victims of the technological inventions we couldn't prevent ourselves from creating or "revealing"? Every discussion about how to rescue democracy that takes aim at "bad actors" overlooks the true gravity of the situation and squanders the chance to perhaps find some sort of way out by pondering technology's increasing constraints upon us. The real problem is not morally dubious big-data companies. It's the fact that knowledge can be deployed to serve a variety of interests and does not inevitably lead to something positive. What's true for nuclear fission is equally true for psychometric personality analysis, and even, since humankind has been able to manipulate DNA, for biology. The dilemma of digitalization is the

outgrowth of the universal law of the insatiability of knowledge and the unavoidability of its use.[28]

Revealing by Metaphors

In his essay "The Question concerning Technology" Heidegger noted that technicians weren't exactly predestined to understand the essence of technology. "Because the essence of technology is nothing technological, essential reflection upon technology and decisive confrontation with it must happen in a realm that is, on the one hand, akin to the essence of technology and, on the other, fundamentally different from it"—so Heidegger writes in this essay. Art, Heidegger continues, is one such realm. But that doesn't rule out science. What is crucial in the search for the essence of technology is not the aesthetic perspective, but a questioning one. That's why Heidegger concludes his essay with the assertion "Questioning is the piety of thought."[29]

At the same time, Heidegger doesn't invoke art by accident. Beyond the contextualization and reduction inherent in non-aesthetic processes of understanding, art allows for a special form of taking in the world. Thus art is a privileged realm in terms of the appearance of the essence of technology. As he says in his essay "The Origin of the Work of Art": "In the work of art, the truth of the being has set itself to work."[30] In other words, the extra significance residing in the "aesthetic vacillation of the signifier" allows art to avoid automatic ways of understanding and conventional forms of reason and to open up new perspectives on its subject matter, including technology.[31] Insofar as this vacillation, this extra significance, can be transferred to examining technology from the perspective of cultural and media studies, that examination should also be able to uncover the essence of technology.

We need to open our thoughts to nonconceptual, metaphorical, and narrative reflections beyond methodological and terminological restrictions. Two good examples are Adorno's essay "The Essay as Form" and Hans Blumenberg's writings on the paradigm of nonconceptuality and metaphorology. The basic assumption of the current book is that our salvation lies in intellectual experiments including speculation and wit, which was characterized by the nineteenth-century German author Jean Paul as the "priest" in the realm of thought that "weds every couple" by discovering commonalities in diverse and distant poles. In this sense, the essays in this book circle about their subject matter as though it were a sculpture, observing it from a variety of vantage points and creating unexpected connections and associations. The goal of this shifting of perspectives is to create a "see change" that doesn't stop at the face value of digital technology.

THE DEATH ALGORITHM AND OTHER DIGITAL DILEMMAS

1   BULLSHIT AND FAST FOOD

[handwritten note: Bullshit = empty talk]

When Donald Trump promises to "make America great again," it's not a lie; it's bullshit. The difference resides in the point of view of the purveyor. The liar knows the truth and knowingly suppresses it. For example, when Trump claimed to have lost hundreds of friends in the 9/11 attacks, he was consciously lying in an attempt to gain some sympathy in the US presidential election. By contrast, when he proclaims that he's "making America great again" or "putting America first," he's nothing but an honest-to-goodness bullshitter. In his heart of hearts, he believes that he knows where America's truest problem lies and how to solve it. Bullshit deceives people with empty talk, not distortions. It is without substance and, as feces, free of any nutritional value. If we shift the metaphor higher up in the human anatomy, we could also call bullshit mental fast food. It contains a huge number of "empty calories" and is as unhealthy and addictive as French fries.[1] Trump is not only the world's most famous bullshitter, he is also its most obvious one. A far less obvious bullshitter is the person who perhaps aspires to become Trump's successor and who is in other respects Trump's polar opposite: Facebook founder Mark Zuckerberg.[2]

BILLIONAIRE PRESIDENTS

Trump has promised to build a wall; Zuckerberg wants to connect people. Trump made his mark with confrontation and isolationism, Zuckerberg with requests for friendship. Trump sees the mainstream media as his archenemy, while Zuckerberg offers them a forum on Facebook. Trump is a loudmouthed entertainer, racist, and sexist, whereas Zuckerberg is a boringly predictable nerd and faithful spouse. Can there be a greater contrast between these two men, who even earned their money in radically different ways? Sometimes it seems as though the only thing they have in common is a complete lack of political experience.

A President Zuckerberg would be a corrective to Trump and would, in many respects, continue the legacy of President Obama. Zuckerberg's motto is not "America first"—by which Trump of course means only some Americans. Zuckerberg's focus is the whole world. Zuckerberg would not present himself as a savior from crisis, but rather as guarantor of continued progress. Like all believers in technology, he's entirely convinced that we live in the best of all possible times and are headed toward even better ones. In his mind, the increase in knowledge thanks to big data and artificial intelligence promises not only to eradicate deadly diseases, but to free up new resources and services for a good life to be had by all.

The preconditions are that human beings continue to network not only within cities and nations, but within a global community, and that the members of this community are all transparent to one another. The central means to this end is Zuckerberg's company Facebook, which would seem to make him supremely qualified to be president in an age of globalization. Zuckerberg is neither shy nor modest in this regard, as is shown by his manifesto "Building Global Community" of February 2017. In it, he depicts Facebook's desire to expand its number of accounts as part of a mission to create a worldwide brotherhood of humankind.[3]

The problem with Zuckerberg's missionary rhetoric is not that it seeks to portray the desire for profits as altruistic. Zuckerberg is, of course, well known for trying to destroy or swallow up rival networks instead of treating them as partners in his cosmopolitan project. And naturally, Zuckerberg himself knows that his company, from its very inception, has been dependent on expansion and doing away with all competition for his users' attention, no matter how many charitable causes his private philanthropic foundation may support. The problem is that Zuckerberg naïvely assumes that transparency automatically leads to understanding and interconnectivity to tolerance, and that the social and cultural problems of globalization can be approached as technological challenges.

ENLIGHTENED CITIZENS

At first glance, everything seems fine. It's true that Facebook connects more and more people who hardly know one another and would have otherwise never gotten a glimpse into other people's lives. It's also true that a great variety of interest and victims groups have formed on the platform and that untold numbers of people discuss political, social, and philosophical questions there. It's true as well that, as Zuckerberg wrote in his manifesto when discussing what he called a "civically engaged community," Facebook has made it easier for people to register to vote and has created a direct feedback loop between politicians and their constituents. Finally, it's true, too, that citizens are better informed about the processes of political decision making when governments publish draft laws and the minutes of meetings online.

But is it really true that Facebook defines its function as activating discourse and solving conflicts of interest by deepening dialogue between participants? On precisely this issue, Zuckerberg's manifesto is as vague as it can be. On the one hand, that document evenhandedly praises the political movements that began on Facebook, be they the Tea Party after Obama's inauguration or the Women's March after Trump's. On the other, the manifesto emphasizes that most conversations on Facebook are "social not ideological." Ignoring the naïve proposition that what is social is not ideological, let's examine the examples Zuckerberg offers: friends having fun, updates from family members, and advice shared in parents' or medical patients' groups. How does this square with Zuckerberg's confidence that the Facebook community can have a positive influence on the world by presenting a diversity of ideas and strengthening mutual understanding? Diversity of fun and educational tips? Mutual understanding among people who share the same hobby or disease? Can a global community superseding all cultural conflict be created by communicating without any political conversations?

Zuckerberg suggested as much when he declared on the margins of a UN meeting in September 2015: "A 'like' or a post won't stop a tank or a bullet, but when people are connected, we have a chance to build a common global community with a shared understanding."[4] His premise is obviously that connection creates understanding rather than underscoring differences and creating conflict. Zuckerberg states this idea more precisely in his manifesto: "Research suggests the best solutions for improving discourse may come from getting to know each other as whole people instead of just opinions—something Facebook may be uniquely suited to do. If we connect with people about what we have in common—sports teams, TV shows, interests—it is easier to have dialogue about what we disagree on. When we do this well, we give billions of people the ability to share new perspectives while mitigating the unwanted effects that come with any new medium."[5]

This holistic view is congenial—human beings truly are more than the sum of their opinions. Who hasn't discovered over a beer after watching a football game that one of the other team's supporters is, despite his differing allegiances, a "pretty good guy after all"? But the only beer on Facebook is in the photos posted by partiers. What's worse, Facebook creates conditions for communication that devalue the mutual drink after a football match or an argument. And that's precisely where the problem starts.

SELF-DELUSION INSTEAD OF SELF-CRITICISM

Zuckerberg's manifesto is most interesting when he expresses his concern about filter bubbles and fake news and admits that social media tend toward simplification, sensationalism, and polarization. Is this supposed to be self-critical? If so, we would also expect the Facebook founder to ask the question that sociologists, media theorists, and other observers have long been posing: is Facebook part of the solution or part of the problem? Perhaps it's understandable that since this question would call his whole manifesto into question, Zuckerberg tries to rhetorically defuse what he cannot ignore. It's not that he wants to deceive his readers. He just wants to win them over to his own optimism. And if it takes a few empty calories to do so, then so be it.

Zuckerberg's self-deception begins with the attempt to see something positive in what is obviously a bad situation. He writes in his manifesto: "Social media is a short-form medium where resonant messages get amplified many times. This rewards simplicity and discourages nuance. At its best, this focuses messages and exposes people to different ideas. At its worst, it oversimplifies important topics and pushes us towards extremes." That's Zuckerberg's argument. But he himself seems to shy away from the presumptiveness of his own relativistic logic, noting in the very next sentence that polarization is indeed a problem. Everywhere we look, he argues, "sensationalism moves people away from balanced nuanced opinions towards polarized extremes." Nonetheless, he claims that this problem is not restricted to social media and fortunately, in a complete whitewash of the situation, that "there are clear steps we can take to correct these effects." All you have to do is unleash the algorithms.

These arguments are symptomatic of the pseudo-logic with which Zuckerberg tries to woo his audience. He relates: "We noticed some people share stories based on sensational headlines without ever reading the story. In general, if you become less likely to share a story after reading it, that's a good sign the headline was sensational. If you're more likely to share a story after reading it, that's often a sign of good in-depth content." If communication is reduced (not to say polarized) that easily, then an additional line of programming code in Facebook's operational system might indeed offer a solution. If read but not shared, then sensationalist. If read and shared, then balanced. *too simple*

Zuckerberg treats sensationalism as an attempt at fraud that can be unmasked and eradicated. As if there weren't legions of people who purposely share sensationalist material precisely because it's sensationalist! As if people weren't already wary of sharing "solid" material since posts that take time to understand tend not to get liked! That brings us back to the fundamental problem, the one of Facebook's own making: the conditions that platform imposes on its "global community." Facebook is by no means the victim of sensationalism, fake news, and filter bubbles. Nor is it a likely remedy. It is—for three reasons—the main source of these three evils.

ENGAGEMENT ON FACEBOOK

The first reason is that Facebook earns money by peddling public attention to advertisers. Thus the ultimate goal is not politically informed citizens but satisfied users. What users want to see, they're given, and not just because Facebook doesn't want to impose its own values. One manager for the platform says: "Our aim is to deliver the types of stories we've gotten feedback that an individual person most wants to see. We do this not only because we believe it's the right thing but also because it's good for our business. When people see content they are interested in, they are more likely to spend time on News Feed and enjoy their experience."[6] Another insider, a former Facebook manager, was even more blunt, saying: "[Facebook's] news feed optimizes for engagement ... bullshit is highly engaging."[7]

Facebook's business model demands, above all, entertaining content that makes people feel at home and keeps them amused. It favors sensationalism over not just what is factually correct but also what is complex, complicated, and potentially boring. It aims to maintain the filter bubble of what people are already accustomed to and not to challenge them with unusual perspectives. For Facebook, "news" and "engagement" are synonymous with "amusement," as free of political significance as fast food is of nutrients. Facebook's stated mission of forming a global community can only be a by-product. For a company listed on the stock market, the bottom line is the bottom line.

The second reason that Facebook is often a force for ill in the world is that the platform's functional logic that determines how users communicate gives us every reason to doubt it will encourage better understanding between people. This logic includes the paradigm of dualistic reaction of likes and dislikes, the populist dominance of the greatest number as a measure of worth without any other justification, the short spans of time posts are examined and evaluated, and the tendency of the Facebook algorithms to form filter bubbles that keep users comfortable. These are hardly the conditions under which balanced political opinions are formed. On the contrary, they encourage spontaneous, emotional partisanship without any sort of critical reflection. The habits that are practiced with reference to completely banal posts, day by day, click by click, influence how people deal with serious information as well. The private—from cat videos to selfies to food porn—has become political in a new, worrisome way.

The third reason Facebook is more a threat than a salvation is that it threatens the development of independent-thinking, well-informed citizens because it attacks the most important bastion of independent thinking and good information. Having become de facto the world's biggest "newspaper," the social network undermines the basis for the existence of quality journalism by siphoning off subscribers and advertisers. Facebook may offer traditional newspapers immediate access to its users via the instant article feature, but this is hardly a gesture of solidarity among like-minded entities. It's an invitation to suicide. How can journalists who try to report in balanced fashion hope to compete with the banality and sensationalism of other Facebook posts? How can Zuckerberg, who stresses how important "a strong news industry" is for forming an "informed community," believe that Facebook's dubious cocktail of attention-grabbing posts is a healthy environment for this end? Trump has declared the mainstream media to be the enemy of the people. Zuckerberg makes the people into the enemy of mainstream media, insofar as the latter don't come around to the sensationalist aesthetic people have come to expect on Facebook.

Zuckerberg's mission of creating a global community is not only vague. If we're talking about an enlightened, tolerant world community, Facebook undermines it in a variety of ways. To turn a blind eye to this is to be prepared to accept the filter bubble as the condition for mutual understanding, as Zuckerberg ultimately suggests.

A WORLD COMMUNITY OF FILTER BUBBLES

When the discussion turns to the values that serve as the basis for why Facebook users should be shown certain content, Zuckerberg rightly points out that there are differences not just between cultures but within every individual culture. Facebook's solution to this question has been to encourage a "system of personal control over our experience." Zuckerberg proclaims: "The idea is to give everyone in the community options for how they would like to set the content policy for themselves. Where is your line on nudity? On violence? On graphic content? On profanity? What you decide will be your personal settings."[8]

Supporting user autonomy rather than taking on the role of censor sounds good in principle. Nonetheless, the question is whether Zuckerberg is not undermining his own project of going beyond the historical progression "from tribes to cities to nations" by creating a global community under Facebook's leadership. Does he not have a responsibility to elevate the process of mutually negotiating normative values to a communicative context beyond that of cultures and nations, instead of allowing every individual to set his or her own values and thus create a variant of the filter bubble?

What seems inconsistent on second glance, once again appears correct on the third. By treating human beings as biological entities and giving them the chance to decide for themselves, independent of their cultural contexts and belief and value systems, Zuckerberg avoids imposing his universal values from on high upon his world community. "Every man must go to heaven in his own way," the Prussian king Friedrich the Great once remarked on the religious confession of his subjects. Much the same thinking inspires Zuckerberg's decision to allow individuals to set the filters of their communication without any group pressure. But on the fourth glance, this is precisely the problem.

This sort of "self-governance," as Zuckerberg calls it in his manifesto, is often criticized as an instance of Western hegemony or even "human rights imperialism." In other cultures, individualism is by no means as highly regarded as in the strongholds and catchment areas of the enlightenment. Before the new world community has even been defined, Zuckerberg organizes it according to Western values and becomes entrapped, without realizing it, in the aporia with which the discourse of human rights has been struggling for decades.

Essentially, Zuckerberg only exacerbates a situation for which other world cultures criticize the West: all-powerful consumer culture. Not only does Facebook surround and load all forms of communication on the platform with advertisements. If it's left up to the individual or the algorithm to choose from a spectrum of information on offer what best suits that individual, then the consumer mentality is determining even the realm of communication. From a critical perspective, what Zuckerberg terms "self-governance" and the specialists in the IT industry call "customization" is actually hyperconsumerism. Nothing underscores this point as well as Zuckerberg's statement: "A squirrel dying in your front yard may be more relevant to your interests right now than people dying in Africa."[9]

No matter what term we use, the urgent question is whether a global community can really be created on the basis of the radical individualism that Facebook not only doesn't correct, but actively encourages.

MCWORLD AND FACEBOOK

In 1995, the American political scientist Benjamin R. Barber published his book *Jihad vs. McWorld*, whose cover featured a woman in a burqa holding a can of Pepsi. That image was itself a thesis. People can drink Pepsi but otherwise remain connected to orthodox tradition. The globalization of Western products doesn't automatically entail the universalization of Western values. Can this insight be applied to Facebook? Is there a structural difference between the mutual love of various cultures for fast food and for a form of communication on a social-media platform? Is a common interest in sensationalist and banal posts a better basis for the world community than a common weakness for saturated fats and sugar?

We can develop the fast-food metaphor further philosophically, if we understand empty calories as lack of substance. This is the basis of the concept of community put forward by French philosopher Jean-Luc Nancy. For Nancy, the global community is not grounded in mutual characteristics like language, culture, religion, or nationality, which all create a sense of togetherness by excluding others. The global community derives its sense from the "sharing of Being" as the "ecstasy of sharing."[10] Viewing Facebook as a site of ecstasy seems reasonable since Nancy identifies in "chatter" what he calls "being-with." He also emphasized that language "right down to those 'phatic,' insignificant remarks ('hello,' 'hi,' 'good' ...) which only sustain the conversation itself—exposes the with, exposes itself as the with, inscribes and ex-scribes itself in the with until it is exhausted, emptied of signification."[11]

"Exhausted and emptied of signification." Though written eight years before the founding of Facebook, are there any better words than these for the platform's culture of communication? Nancy's objection to the metaphysical foundation of previous conceptions of community reads like a theoretical anticipation of the practice on Facebook. Connection for connection's sake, "being with," sharing and self-sustainment—is mere self-celebration in fact the best basis for a global community?

From this perspective, Facebook is both the practice complementing the theory and the triumph of technology over culture, since it is technology that forges hundreds of millions of users from diverse cultures into a community, "our community," as Zuckerberg's manifesto calls it. But the triumph of technology is also a trick of the West to get the whole world on its side without being accused of imperialism, reconfiguring it to conform to the model of the narcissistic, consumption-obsessed, entertainment-addicted superficial individual. Insofar as technology expresses the society that invented it, its spread always simultaneously entails the exporting of a culture. Telephones encourage dialogue, for instance, while microwave ovens help maintain the frenetic pace of modernity. If computer codes as well as laws determine our actions, then globalized software and hardware influences value systems all over the world.

The change wrought upon culture by technology doesn't preclude technology occasionally adapting to the details of different cultures. There are mobile phones for Muslims that remind users when it's time to pray, point out the direction of Mecca, and block calls for the subsequent twenty minutes. Nonetheless, without spreading any explicit propaganda, Facebook is bringing narcissism to all corners of the globe just as the selfie stick is transforming every attraction into a bit of background for self-staging. In the same vein, Napster made peer-to-peer sharing (or, if you prefer, piracy) of music possible across the world, and online dating has become popular even in those places where it isn't a social necessity. "Do you want to sell sugar water for the rest of your life, or do you want to come with me and change the world?" was the question Apple boss Steve Jobs used to hire away John Scully, the head of Pepsi. And whereas sugar and saturated fats merely reshape the bodies of individuals, Facebook's fast food changes the corpus of society and may be capable of creating the basis of a global community that is actually based on nothing.

DIALECTIC SHORT CIRCUIT

Advocates of Western culture don't like adjectives like *narcissistic*, *consumerist*, or *entertainment-addicted*. Many theories that seek to rehabilitate Western culture try to reverse the cutting edge of such negative terms by celebrating the emptiness of the postmodern subject as freedom from ideological and religious hysteria. The egocentric, politically disinterested subject, defenders argue, is a guarantor of and not a threat to democracy because democracy is the basis for living a life of narcissism. In this view, egotism negates peer pressure, hedonism functions as a shield against ideology, and consumerism becomes "pragmatic cosmopolitanism." If we take this logic to an extreme, every Hollywood blockbuster with confident, consumer-oriented women characters is an argument against the horror of female genital mutilation.[12]

There are indeed good reasons to promote radical self-development without any religious or philosophical self-reflection or experience. The superficial subject, after all, is also one who is indifferent to questions of deeper meaning and collective narratives and takes no personal affront at opposing norms of behavior and values—to say nothing of mobilizing people for Jihad, if his or her faith is under assault. Twenty years before Zuckerberg's manifesto on "global community," the first advocates of the "digital nation" were described as tolerant and generous precisely because they were postpolitical and indifferent.[13] This subject no longer purports to possess the truth, to say nothing of wanting to make the world a better place. So does this mean that Zuckerberg is on the right track with his plan to transform the human race into a community of individuals beyond any political persuasion and cultural boundaries?

To think that would be to overlook the fact that hypermodern, late capitalist, neoliberal society so greatly releases the individual from traditional cultural and social ties that—depending on the individual's economic situation and psychological constitution—he or she may also feel lost. In that case, people are less apt to attempt to network with the world in the abstract sense Zuckerberg describes than to seek the feeling of belonging Facebook offers directly with its group pages and indirectly with its filter algorithms. The result is new borders that are even stricter since in the realm of online communication, trolls and social bots relentlessly promote the "self" and attack the "other" with extreme vitriol. The protective shadows of Internet anonymity make it easy to shitstorm people—and hard to develop the sort of good will toward someone else that often accompanies the beer after a disagreement.

Indifference should not be mistaken for tolerance. We tolerate when we endure difference, not when we merely ignore others. To strengthen the unbound "we" of humanity against the "we" of nations, cultures, and other forms of belonging, it's not sufficient to free all the "Is" from their group constraints and release them into their own filter bubbles thanks to a "system of personal control over our experience." The global community presumes that it knows itself in all its facets and thus must restrict individuals' freedom to decide about their own lives whenever that freedom butts up against knowledge about the lives of others.

The utopia of universal understanding cannot be realized by excluding everything that threatens to draw borders. Understanding begins with the acceptance of difference, with agreeing to disagree—which also entails searching together for consensus and not accusing one another of lies. Facebook hinders this search because it drowns potentially explosive differences of opinion in everyday banalities and sensationalism, because personal information management is allowed to create filter bubbles, and because the expansion of the corporation deprives quality journalism, which traditionally preserved difference and communicated diverse information, of its existential basis.

FAST-FOOD RHETORIC

Zuckerberg's manifesto positions Facebook as a political savior in times when the European Union's primary ambition is once again to function as an economic bloc, the battle of cultures is making itself felt in terrorist attacks in the world's metropolises, and for many people the Internet has become a dystopia. Zuckerberg would like to weave a narrative of Facebook as the friendly face of the web, but given Facebook's business interests, it's reasonable to accuse the platform's founder of hypocrisy and see in his manifesto a transparent tactic to deflect the increasing criticism Facebook has come under after Trump's electoral victory. In any case, Zuckerberg's narrative is naïve and without substance. And the problem isn't just Facebook, but Zuckerberg himself.

If Zuckerberg were more interested in the problem for which he proposes Facebook as the solution, he might be able to develop thesis that would inspire the stagnant discussions of experts, making them take up the topics of melting pots and multiculturalism, pluralism, and cosmopolitanism. Nancy's concept of community is one starting point; the promise of a world community created by technology is another. We need to ask: does the use of Facebook, as a practice that shapes culture and the McWorld of cyberspace, create a "vernacular cosmopolitanism" or "cosmopolitanism from below"? Does the model of interconnected Facebook groups conform to the hybrid one of "patriotic cosmopolitanism"?[14]

The main objection to Zuckerberg is not that he doesn't have any better solution to the issue of global community than the experts in the multiculturalism and cosmopolitanism debate. It is not even that Facebook defines popularity via likes, shares, and visits, and thereby promotes dualistic thinking, numerical populism, and filter bubbles. Social networks, we must admit, are ultimately also victims of the technological environment whose logic of connection and calculation are imminent in the names of its two main components: the Internet and computers.

The main objection to Zuckerberg is that he thinks he can solve a massively complex problem of universal human rights and global community with a technological quick fix—without any knowledge of the discussions concerning this issue or any reflection about whether technological answers are even suited to these questions. The very first premise of Zuckerberg's manifesto—that there was no controversy surrounding attempts to form a global community when Facebook started out—is utter nonsense. This might be the way the circle of engineers, with whom Zuckerberg surrounds himself, feels. But if he'd asked around outside his own filter bubble, he would have realized how heated the formation of a global community has been discussed since the late twentieth century. Zuckerberg seems entirely unaware of the people who—fifteen years ago, in an age when everything was still thought possible on the Internet—envisioned how cosmopolitanism would develop with respect to the web and prophesied that a common culture would grow out of our common use of technology.[15]

What President Trump was forced to admit after his reckless promise to dismantle the Affordable Health Care Act might someday apply to a possible President Zuckerberg as well: who would have thought that the creation of a global community would be so difficult? And the answer he'll be given will be the same one that Trump got on health care. Everybody who's ever stopped to think a bit about the matter knew that it was difficult. Zuckerberg publically and unapologetically admits to his "engineering mindset," which leads him to believe that any system, including social ones, can be improved.[16] But Facebook's contribution to improving how people inform themselves politically is, at the very least, ambivalent. When we're talking about the creation of a global community, merely linking people is not enough. The important questions are: how and to what end? Otherwise, you might as well say that French fries and ketchup are part of a healthy diet because they're made of tomatoes and potatoes. And that would truly be bullshit.

how and why are we linking ppl?

They've become part of everyday life: People who stare at their mobile phones not just when they're sitting in the subway, but while they're walking around the city. Human beings whose "ambient attention" extends only as far as the next obstacle. Any resistance we may mount to such smartphone zombies, or "smombies"—for instance, by defiantly getting in their way as they plod through overcrowded streets—is as futile as it is aggressive. True smombies can avoid running into other people without taking their eyes off their mobile devices. The only consolation is that little bit of schadenfreude we feel when, completely distracted from the real world, they get off the elevator on the wrong floor or head into a bathroom for the opposite sex.

In Hong Kong, where I've lived for a few years, almost every second person is a smombie. Nowhere else have I observed so many people walking through a city with their eyes glued to their cell phones as in this Asian metropolis, despite the great numbers of pedestrians jostling for space on its narrow sidewalks. Amusingly outdated prerecorded warnings can be heard everywhere on subway escalators: "Please hold the hand rail. Don't keep your eyes only on the mobile phone!" Subway escalators are perhaps the only places where pedestrians' obsession with their phones doesn't actually represent a hazard, and guardians of public safety would be pleased if those were the only places they were used.

But this problem has arrived even in quaint little towns in Switzerland. In May 2015, police in Lausanne attracted attention with a video warning against the potential consequences of sending text messages while walking. "The Mobile Phone in Traffic Trick" is the title of the public service clip. It features a twenty-four-year-old rap and R'n'B fan named Jonas who likes to chat with his friends while on the move. "Jonas doesn't know a thing about magic," a narrator says. "But he's about to disappear. Let's take a closer look." The audience watches as Jonas starts to cross a street while texting. He glances in the wrong direction and gets swept out of the picture frame by a car speeding the opposite way. People scream, and the other pedestrians look horrified. Then the narrator, who turns out to be a mortuary owner, ironically signs off with the words: "See you soon!"[1]

WASTE OF SPACE

The police stage the smombie phenomenon as the sort of fatal traffic accident with which they are all too familiar. But the actual disappearing act happens long before the car smashes into the distracted pedestrian. Smombies treat the distance between point A and point B as merely a stretch of time and remove themselves mentally from the physical world to the parallel universe of social networks. In this sense, they are gone even though they remain physically present. Smombies are not the undead returning from the grave, but rather the mentally absent who leave their bodies behind.

Is this what irritates us, assuming we are in fact irritated, by seeing people lost in their mobile devices all around us? Do we tacitly hope for someone to interact with us and thus feel disappointed when everyone withdraws so radically? Do we resent them for the solitude they force upon us? Or is it merely aggravating that they have the temerity to expect *us* to get out of *their* way?

It's perhaps less self-pitying to understand smombies' rejection of others as a consequence of media history. Smartphones complete the disappearance of space that began, at the latest, with the advent of modern transportation. The landscape may have rushed by in a blur outside the windows of a train, but it is gone completely when we look out of an airplane. People are suddenly able to travel halfway around the world without ever seeing anything but airports. Bridging distances no longer means encountering space, as anyone who takes the subway in a big city knows. Fundamentally, even a horse-drawn carriage entailed a betrayal of space since it allowed the passenger to withdraw from it, for instance, into the world of a book. As Johann Gottfried Seume, the most famous walker in German literary history, proposed around 1800, the pedestrian is the only one who truly experiences his environment because he can always sit down on a rock at the edge of a field and ask passersby for directions.

Now, with the existence of mobile media and social networks, even pedestrians no longer have to encounter their surroundings. People wearing <u>Walkmen</u> may have strode around in their own worlds to an extent, <u>but at least</u> they saw the world they no longer wished to hear. By contrast, smartphones reduce space to a distance to a certain destination. Intermediary space is only an interval of time that is actually spent elsewhere: in a social network, on a computer game, on a website, or in a chat with friends. The screens in our hands, like the carriage, the car, the subway, and the train, cause space to disappear. The smartphone is a vehicle.

PLACELESSNESS

Vehicle = non-place

A vehicle is what French anthropologist Marc Augé calls a "non-place," akin to shopping centers, highways, and train stations.[2] While they are not places devoid of meaning or characteristics, they are—in contrast to a corner bar in New York or a bistro in Paris—places without history. Their specifics do not develop onsite but are rather imposed globally as a formula. And just like train stations, trains themselves are non-places. The train from Berlin to Munich is neither Prussian nor Bavarian, which is why it can be used equally well to travel from cosmopolitan Hanseatic city of Hamburg to the quaint southwestern German town Freiburg the very next day. Every form of technology is an inhabitable place with its own special culture—McLuhan calls it the "message" of the medium, Heidegger the "essence" of technology.[3] That also goes for pieces of technology we can hold in our hands.

Technology, be it a carriage, a car, a train, or a smartphone, may create non-places, but this process is only temporary and happens more literally than Augé describes. The smartphone transforms surrounding space into a place that really doesn't exist for people who, engrossed by cyberspace, don't register the cultural specifics of their environment: the structure of the doors of buildings, the graffiti on the walls, the residents, or the special quality of light on a broad street lined with sycamore trees. Space always entails time in the sense of duration. Architectural styles, street names, monuments, and also the destinies entailed by a white rock, the bent slats of a bench, or vehicles making their way on a road—these are all phenomena of times past that space makes appear present to us.

This memory space accompanies the corporeal time. Human beings also preserve the time that psychologically and physically determines us, in everything from the music and books we encounter in our youths to the scars from our first operations or the furrows and wrinkles on our faces with age. When a human being enters a space, instead of merely rushing through it, two biographies encounter one another. Moreover, when a human being is on the go, time moves in space. Human beings are systems of coagulated culture that they bring from point A to point B and leave behind everywhere in between, wherever contact is made with those who live in one place, their progeny, and anyone who follows in their tracks. That is why places in traffic hubs and on trade routes—for instance, the Silk Road or Venice—are so vivid and full of meaning.

We sense this synthesis of space and time when we visit foreign cities' cathedrals and squares and ask what they have to tell us about those specific places' past. Very few of us can resist going to such locations. Tourists traditionally feel a responsibility after having traveled from point A to point B to be able to tell the people in point A what point B was like. But even this behavior is no longer a given. Today people often just post photos to networks of friends who don't expect any further information upon the travelers' return. Space disappears not only when people rush through it without a glance but also when they document it blindly.

THE AVOIDANCE OF CHANCE

Is this an instance of envying the long past of space, which makes our own futures appear terrifyingly short, or is it the desire to take vengeance on everything that will outlive us which encourages us to flee space for the parallel world of mobile devices? Or is it just the fear of the unknown that space offers us? Is the loss of space an incidental by-product of the attempt to avoid chance?

One banal form of this denial or loss is the way GPS navigation robs us of orientation. "In twenty meters, turn left!" What do we know about a space we encounter in this way? Could we retrace our steps if our device lost satellite contact or its battery ran out? In that case, we would find ourselves back in space, forced to orient ourselves around street signs and buildings. We might have to ask others for directions. We would get a feel for our environment. Our problem is that we tend to follow suggestions made by an app rather than go down a street that looks interesting. Our problem is that we've handed over the power to determine how we encounter space—from the routes we take to the locales (stores, restaurants) we frequent—to technology and the people behind it. Every encounter that is mediated by new technologies initially interposes itself between us and the object to which those technologies are, according to their own logic, connecting us.

No less significant is the loss we undergo when we know a space well and decide, for precisely that reason, to depart from it—when we cheat ourselves not of alternative routes but of alternative experiences. Smombies enact a popular referendum against chance. By staring at their smartphones, they withdraw from the alternatives of space, which may generously send some people or another across their paths, in the hope of starting a conversation, a friendship, or even eventually a marriage. The smartphone becomes the place of chance, in which apps like happn show users which members of certain social networks happen to be in the vicinity. But GPS-based apps organize and doubly constrain chance. For every person we may "encounter" in this fashion, we can check how much we have in common before mounting a "private" approach that the other person will only see if he or she does exactly the same thing.

This app describes itself as a mere social aid: "It all starts in real life." The company's Internet video shows how people happn brings together encounter each other in real space. But the app that acts as though it's only a technological support for chance is essentially a colonization of it. If an app and not space is the mediator, the culture of those who provide the app determines the encounter. That expresses itself both in the interface that the app provider gives to users to allow them to communicate and in the advertisements with which this communication is surrounded. Anyone who wants to see whom he or she is encountering every day must first see what there is to buy. It is the reversal of the already-reversed situation of an encounter in a real-life market in which one person goes shopping and ends up meeting a love interest by chance.

It's hardly surprising that this app would try to deflect users' attention to commercial ends. After all, this is the whole raison d'être of most apps and social networks that offer their services for free. Nonetheless, this instance of a company monetarizing and capitalizing on human eye contact neatly illustrates where most of the attention withdrawn from real space ultimately ends up. The technologizing of chance diverts our attention to the benefit of consumer culture. Do we take offense at smombies because we believe they're collaborating—unwittingly, passively, or perhaps even actively—with this capitalist model?

THE END OF TRAVEL

"People who only know their own world will think it is the only one there is"—that's one way of formulating what Oscar Wilde called the "dogmatism of the untraveled."[4] The politically significant promise of traveling is that we will gain tolerance of others and reflexive distance from our own world, and no one knows better than great writers that we don't have to go abroad to experience what is foreign. It can also be accomplished by reading books that introduce us to other worlds or by walking in urban space where a variety of worlds collide. Traveling in this sense isn't a matter of kilometers but the encounters that happen along the way. If difference is only perceived as a shadowy obstacle in our "ambient attention," there are no such encounters. The city loses the cosmopolitan potential that distinguishes it from the conservatism of small towns.

This sort of loss can also happen when the virtual parallel world is a social network. More often than not, despite their global structure, such networks are nothing more than villages in which everyone knows everyone and all think alike, and which only admit outsiders if they assimilate into what is familiar. The filter bubble of being among one's "own" kind negates the possibility offered by public space for personal growth by taking in the completely different experiences and perspectives of the people we happen to encounter. The problem is not the network itself, but how it is generated by means of agreement, liking, and comparing. The problem is the eradication of others. The fate of all communication in cyberspace is to become the object of analysis, monitoring, and consequently optimization in all its various form.

Even that space where people have previously interacted with the world most intensively and primarily is subject to this threat. If online campuses and learning software become the norm, as profit-oriented IT companies and shortsighted politicians hope they will someday, schools and universities will cease to exist as a place of direct encounters and spontaneous experiences. Not only will the solidarity of traditional school classes and learning groups disappear, so too will the unplanned acquaintances we make at the concerts, readings, open-mic events, and political discussions we happen to attend. We will lose the possibilities for encountering others and experiencing the world in ways that go beyond immediate shared interests and course schedules.

The problem is the algorithms that optimize our capacity for choice, which always followed its own leanings. The more human interaction happens digitally, the more effectively algorithms eradicate chance, and it is no accidental paradox of our times that occasional attempts are made to use algorithms themselves to solve the problem. Algorithms can even be designed to encourage chance. If they so desire, people can let algorithms determine where they'll be living next month, what locales they will frequent, and which people they will meet. But only superficially does this seem like an instance of people using technology to regain what once, in the absence of technology, determined their lives. It's actually an example of fitting square pegs in round holes. What can be more absurd than people who want to open themselves up to chance moving through space in precisely the same way as chance-averse smombies and allowing their smartphones to tell them where they can have accidental encounters?[5]

Nonetheless, even programmed chance is better than the absence of it; at least it involves opening ourselves up to things we don't control. Like public space, programmed chance contains the possibility of us becoming more than what we are or think we have to become, the possibility of escaping the filter bubble of what we presume to be our own kind and of going beyond time-killing distractions to discover ourselves. Like public space, programmed chance is a refuge of private life, free from inspection and nudging and free for experience and daring. Is it the thoughtless squandering of this refuge that really irritates us about smombies? The frivolous refusal to explore a deeper reserve of possibilities? The inability to pause and consider things while people are on their way between A and B? The fact that they are running away from themselves?

THE POLITICS OF SPACE

In the 1950s and '60s, you would sometimes see people ambling aimlessly around several of the Western world's biggest cities. They were part of a "situationist" performance aimed at breaking through everyday routine and allowing people to see their more or less familiar surroundings in new ways. The point was to politicize the activity of the *flâneur* and use it to expand people's consciousness. This revolutionary strategy was called the *dérive*, a term coined by the situationist Guy Debord who in his famous 1967 manifesto, *The Society of the Spectacle*, attacked the modern emphasis on entertainment and commercialization.

The *dérive* was intended to interrupt people's usual lives and, when put into practice, to lead to *détournement*, "rerouting" or "hijacking," a kind of oppositional appropriation of cultural objects, concepts, and situations. *Détournement* sought to disrupt the seemingly inherent logic and logical nature of spatial constellation and social interactions in order to critique dominant ideologies. Well-known recent examples include the semiotic kidnappings of Adbuster antiadvertisements or "subvertisements," the politically charged performative pranks of the artist group the Yes Men, and the 18,000 naked people American photographer Spencer Tunick assembled on May 6, 2015, on the world's third-largest city square, the Zócalo at the heart of arch-Catholic Mexico City.

When thousands of Mexican men and women (not counting the tourists who joined the action in solidarity) disrobe in front of the massive edifices of state power (the Metropolitan Cathedral, the National Palace, and the Supreme Court), it is a clear statement against old-fashioned, conservative Mexico. In this action, the Zócalo itself, a traditional spot for sociopolitical demonstrations and proclamations, becomes the object of popular intervention. The unforgettable backdrop it provided for viewers as well as participants was a reminder that any refiguring of the public realm must begin in public.

It's no accident that at a time when media are increasingly interposing themselves into people's interactions with space and other people, political philosophy more and more often equates public space with a place to assemble. The "politics of the street" is a key concept within Judith Butler's "performative theory of assembly," which explores the political potential of physical presence in public space.[6] This entails more than just demonstrating, occupying public parks, or rioting in the streets. It is also about unlocking the potential for unmediated encounters within public space and the uncontrolled energy it can generate. Ultimately, the point is to perceive reality beyond the digital conditions of communication that threatens to filter out Tunick's naked people—and not only them.

No smombie, of course, would be able to cross even the smallest city square and fail to notice if it were full of naked people. But just as the disrobed participants acting in unison on the Zócalo symbolized the voice of the street, smombies symbolize the silencing of that voice. On the symbolic level, the smartphone is a tool of *récupération*, as the situationists called successful defense against *détournement*: the regaining of the power of definition by making the subversive seem banal or isolating those to which it is addressed. Even if people occasionally use smartphones to arrange to meet for political action, they remain lightning rods that divert public energy and make it harmless.

MAKING THINGS DISAPPEAR

The social significance of various media also resides in the disconnection they initiate. If the smartphone separates us from experiencing the space between point A and point B, it again resembles a vehicle—but this time a helicopter rather than a subway or an airliner. It keeps people apart from others whom they might otherwise encounter when they're on the go, for instance, homeless people, UNICEF volunteers, or others soliciting help. In our ambient attention, all these groups are degraded to the status of objects with which we need to avoid colliding. Smombies' lack of attention to their environment may lead to the odd individual being erased from the scene (and screen) by a speeding car. But equally tragic is the precondition of such traffic accidents, the smombies' erasure of their environment: the beggar, the money-collecting activist, the stranger, the traffic light and the car.

We need to ask ourselves where our modern media themselves are leading and what future is entailed by the message they communicate. Anyone familiar with countries in which "gated communities" and domestic security guards are part of middle- and upper-class life, keeping the rest of society at bay, will suspect where all this is headed. The smartphone is the helicopter with which even poor people move through space without encountering it. The power of space is thus wiped out for precisely those who need it most. If we consider the possible consequences of eradicating chance and commercializing communication, it is clear that our self-disempowerment begins with a disinterest in public space.

Of course, people can use smartphones to get information about how to support UNICEF or other aid organizations. Of course, people can remove themselves from their social-media filter bubbles or use social media to join political discussion groups. People always have the option of doing something. The question is whether we *have to* behave in some way toward people with whom we *could* occupy ourselves, as is the case when a beggar or a donation solicitor catches our eye or when chance makes us cross paths with strangers. The question is how many of us do these things if we're given a choice not to.

The smombies' flight from space is a ticking time bomb and could, if we are right about its causes and effects, lead to a future that consists of non-places in which non-people, preoccupied by trivialities, move from point A to point B without seeing anything of whatever remains and probably won't be worth seeing anyway. It is probably this vision of the future that truly angers us when people with mobile phones avoid us without looking up whenever we get in their way.

3 MARSHMALLOW CULTURE

On January 23, 2017, the *New Yorker* ran a cartoon depicting Donald Trump at his inauguration. A man representing the Chief Justice of the Supreme Court extends his hand, which has something in it, and says: "You can eat the one marshmallow right now, or, if you wait fifteen minutes, I'll give you two marshmallows and swear you in as President of the United States."[1] The cartoon calls us back to our childhood: The uncle just showed us a marshmallow and then left the room. If we immediately call him back, we immediately get the marshmallow. If we wait until he returns to the room on his own, we get two marshmallows. The "uncle" was the Austrian-American psychologist Walter Mischel, and the game was part of an experiment he conducted with four-year-old children between 1968 and 1974. In 1980 and 1981, Mischel revisited his subjects and discovered that the ones who were capable of waiting as young children were better developed intellectually and socially than their impatient peers.

The *New Yorker* cartoon presumes that the audience is familiar with the marshmallow experiment as well as with the psychological theories of "present bias" and "instant gratification." These theories hold that human beings favor payoffs that are closer to the present time and don't like to forgo pleasures even in return for future rewards. All of us have our own experience with this sort of shortsightedness, for instance when we vow to give up smoking or eating sweets and resolve to get more exercise. Other sociological analyses carried out around the same time as Mischel's experiment also classify a desire for instant gratification, blind to the future, as a trait of the "narcissistic personality" who "does not accumulate goods and provisions against the future," as we learn, "but demands immediate gratifications and lives in a state of restless, perpetually unsatisfied desire."[2] The idea crops up in the old saying "A bird in hand is worth two in the bush," and also in literature and television, whenever someone makes a pact with the devil and sells his immortal soul for benefits in the here-and-now. This is precisely the pact that the majority of human beings have made with the Internet.

THE CULTURE OF INSTANT GRATIFICATION

In its early days, the Internet was something users had to wait for patiently to get their reward. Indeed, in 1995, the World Wide Web was known as the "world wide wait" because people could brew themselves a pot of coffee in the time it took between when they dialed their providers with their modems and a connection was actually established. Today we have broadband and 5G. No one is willing to wait more than three seconds for anything on the web—that was Mark Zuckerberg's argument in July 2015 for why newspapers should take part in Facebook's "Instant Articles" service, which posts news on the social network in milliseconds. Millennials seem to have little more self-control than children. What isn't immediately accessible is disregarded.

But that goes not just for millennials. In an age of over-abundant information, impatience also influences the behavior of older people to the point that they too will engage in criminal activities. The main reason people download films or music illegally is not a refusal to pay for it but unwillingness to wait until a movie or song is available through a licensed provider—just as people are no longer capable of waiting for the conclusion of a thought that's longer than a tweet. The Internet encourages a culture of "hyper-attention" and "hyper-stimulation" that privileges instant over delayed gratification. The result is that whenever things get complicated, we immediately click on the next bit of entertainment without the slightest ambition to understand what strikes us as difficult. The Internet is a colossal "now machine." On the Internet, adult subjects would scarcely let Uncle Mischel in the door before they grabbed the marshmallow. It's no surprise than the average human attention span is currently estimated at eight seconds—shorter than that of a goldfish.[3]

A glance at a library or classroom confirms the extent of the problem. With gleaming eyes, their textbooks on the table and smartphones in their hands, students scroll through the updates on their social networks, which promise to be much more amusing than the subject matter of the books they are supposed to understand. The new media make it easy to avoid everything difficult. What chance does a book have against Instagram? What are the prospects of a serious newspaper article against a salacious bit of fake news? The reverse side to getting everything you want right now is delaying anything that demands an effort: procrastination and instant gratification go hand in hand, as do present bias and confirmation bias.

The problem has become so acute that many people need outside help, such as the WasteNoTime browser extension, to limit the time they can spend on social networks or their favorite website. This form of self-discipline relies on technical means that pay tribute to the source of the problem in the very moment they solve it. We go for gratification now and leave it to the app to discipline us later.

DIALECTIC OF WISH FULFILLMENT

The commercialization and centralization of communication that leaves users at the mercy of giant private companies and government intelligence services aren't the only things that have gone wrong with the Internet. The main problem is that the Internet gives us everything we want: information to suit our own tastes, entertainment without limits, and satisfaction without delay. The problem is one of control not *over* but *by* the individual. The technical terms for this are "customization" and "filter bubbles," into which the algorithms on Facebook and elsewhere increasingly herd us, often without our knowledge but mostly with our consent. What may look like external control is basically a human impulse asserting itself through technology. Just as we impulsively want the marshmallow, we also feel an impulse to keep certain people and certain views at a distance. The

individual here is the perpetrator, not the victim, which doesn't make the situation any easier.

It's no secret that we are our own worst enemies and that achievement is based on overcoming our natural limitations. For that reason, clever athletes seek out tough coaches and trainers. Children, however, aren't so clever. They get upset when their parents don't allow them to order just French fries or play with their mobile phones in restaurants. Conversely, schoolkids prefer "nice" teachers, while cursing those who make them waste weekends reading texts that are much too long and much too complicated. We only appreciate the wisdom and power of such strict taskmasters in delaying gratification later in life—once we have put the classroom long behind us and understand the entire import of Jenny Holzer's unsettling conceptual art project, the bright-light sign, in the middle of billboards and skyscrapers, saying: "Protect Me from What I Want."

The Internet—together with its lackeys, the mobile and social media—is Pandora's gift for our age. It encourages a culture of immediate gratification in which fun is only a mouse click away. The old adage "without perspiration there is no inspiration" has been long forgotten. The "weaklings," to use a term some athletic instructors might deploy, have won the day. In a physical sense, this weakening expresses itself in our decreasing willingness to wait for even short periods when we're in pain, which, supported by the lobbying of the pharmaceutical industry, has led to the massive abuse of medications, at least in America. In times of dwindling readiness to postpone the fulfillment of our desires, doctors who advocate greater tolerance of pain and professors and journalists who put their faith in complicated books and complex analyses have become little better than irritating spoilsports.

Everything Bad Is Good for You was the title of a groundbreaking book by Steven Johnson from 2005. Its subtitle was *How Today's Popular Culture Is Actually Making Us Smarter*. Johnson's work was a defense of much-maligned pop culture as something actually quite demanding, which the author sought to illustrate using the example of video games and TV series like *The Sopranos* or *The West Wing*. Thirteen years later, however, it is time to turn Johnson's programmatic statement on its head: everything good is bad for you. So-called trash TV, made for viewers who are presumably lowbrow and lower class, may be better than cultural pessimists believe, but the promises of the Internet are also more dangerous than media optimists have been willing to acknowledge. The culture of instant gratification robs us of the endorphins that, in thinking as in sports, are produced only through exertion and endurance. What *feels* good often takes away any chance for us to grow beyond our limitations—as sportspeople, students, or readers.

"You won't know if you like it until you try it," parents sometimes tell young children. How can anyone be induced to try anything in times of antiauthoritarian education and rampant narcissism? We seek to persuade and seduce. The magic formula put forth by today's behavioral researchers and political scientists is called "nudging." People should be nudged toward making correct decisions, whether on questions of nutrition and physical exercise or in education, choosing a partner, or saving for retirement. Nudging seeks to cure the problem of shortsighted behavior patterns by using a refined "decision-making architecture": tax breaks encourage people to take out private pension plans, and salad, not French fries, is placed up front and thus made more readily available in school cafeterias, public facilities, and wherever therapists rather than drug dealers run the show. Nudging uses the power of inertia as a paradoxical update of the marshmallow experiment. What is good is directly obtainable, whereas what is bad takes some effort.

THE NICE LIFE AS THE WRONG LIFE

The fact that the 2017 Nobel Prize for Economics went to Richard Thaler, a scholar who coauthored a book about nudging, underscores the necessity of researching the conditions and possibilities of delayed wish fulfillment in the age of instant gratification. Thaler and his coauthor Cass Sunstein even promote nudging as an answer to the problems of environmental pollution and the shortage of natural resources, opening up a new perspective. The self-denial we are supposed to engage in to create a better future is no longer directly solely toward our own future but that of all humankind, including people who have yet to be born. This paradigm shift highlights the social and political dimension of individuals forgoing immediate wish fulfillment.[4]

The disciplining of the instincts of the stomach that Mischel's experiment encouraged in the four-year-olds is ultimately a basis for ethical behavior. Delaying gratification and curbing one's own nature are preconditions of civilization and progress. Wherever external circumstances produce a challenge, the crucial thing is to withstand impulses and remind oneself of what seems rational in the long term. This applies to a difficult text that promises to give readers a deeper understanding of the world, something threateningly foreign that can open our eyes to the diversity of human existence, or the additional effort required to avoid wasting energy and polluting the environment. Little children aren't the only ones who confront the marshmallow problem. It is the central one of humanity. The second marshmallow contains the prospect of human beings being better able to live together.

Adorno's famous adage "There is no right life in the wrong one" from his 1951 collection of aphorisms and essays *Minima Moralia* challenges readers not to accept an unacceptable status quo. We should not allow ourselves to become accomplices to an unjust world and live a "good" life while all around us people are suffering. Adorno calls upon us to show concern, compassion, and solidarity. It is a call that nonetheless makes a right life—or a "livable" one—in a wrong world seem possible, provided that the center of that life is the future, in an expanded sense, and not the present. The determining criterion is not our own satisfaction now but the satisfaction of all people in a future society yet to be created.[5]

The resistance Adorno calls for in this context must begin "within ourselves." It is directed primarily "against what the world has made of us."[6] For four-year-olds, the world is hardly formed at all. At the same time, they can learn to share sweets or wait until the uncle returns in order to ultimately gain more sweets. No matter whether we're talking about sweets or sociopolitical questions, the struggle against the human impulse to think only of ourselves in the here and now involves issues such as the distribution of wealth, human rights, the problem of refugees, tolerance for those who think differently, and environmental protection. It is about how human beings can live better or at least not worse in the future—as members of society and as inhabitants of planet Earth. Ethical behavior consists of developing an attitude that comes from the future instead of from our own bellies.

Ultimately, the welfare of humankind is a matter of transitioning from "What do I want right now?" to "What is right in the long term?" That presupposes an ability to think ahead while acting in the present and including others in our own concerns. It is a further development of the parental instinct into empathy for our neighbors, compatriots, and foreigners. We need to embrace the world to make something better out of it. The mentality of instant gratification is not only unhealthy; it's unethical. That is the deeper moral of the marshmallow story.

A MARSHMALLOW PRESIDENT

One individual who has nothing whatever to do with this call to change, this ambition, and this desire for progress is Donald Trump—a president with the mental disposition of a four-year-old who sends tweets at 4 a.m. and immediately feels slighted if everything doesn't go his way. The times when he posts his tweets and the grammatical mistakes they contain are an expression of an impulsiveness of a man whose own interests are all that matters, who considers political correctness a form of coercive self-censorship, and who would rather have a hamburger and a Coke ten times over a salad with mineral water.

Trump's populistic outbursts allow his supporters to feel at home in their emotional urges, preventing any sort of self-questioning just as effectively as any filter bubbles on the Internet. They are as intellectually simple as language itself in the multimedia age and operate as shortsightedly and irresponsibly as possible, for instance by promoting coal mining or denying climate change. Trump's refusal to do his homework as president and gain knowledge about policy areas he now controls, instead of spending hours watching television, is understandable to everyone who, in the face of all the sensations material on offer on his or her social networks, also has trouble reading words without pictures or listening to a guest speak for longer than a goldfish.

Thirty-five years after the fact it is clear that Walter Mischel's experiment with human personality did not end before November 2016. The question that remains to be answered is how the four-year-olds' ability to wait back then corresponds to the same people's electoral choices now. That is the deeper punchline in the *New Yorker* cartoon. The magazine's creators and readers know, of course, that Trump is so popular precisely because he's so unable to control his inner urges. Trump supporters praise him for being "natural," "straightforward," and "authentic"—to name just some of the euphemistic adjectives for a person whose knowledge and behavior give no indication that he has ever been able to resist following a momentary impulse.

Trump is the perfect president for the Internet age because he frees his constituents of something of which he himself is incapable and which the Internet doesn't encourage anyway: the self-control to defer gratification. He was inaugurated as president on January 22, 2017, one day before the *New Yorker* cartoon, not despite but precisely because he would never even wait three seconds—to say nothing of fifteen minutes—for a marshmallow.

4 TRAFFIC COPS AND MEDIA EDUCATION

It's no exaggeration to say that the digitalization of society has put enormous pressure on schools. We live in an age when pupils can evaluate their teachers and parents can grade their children's schools on Internet platforms. An age in which college-track students read through the comments of their 100,000 Instagram fans while the teacher in front of the class is saying something about someone called Hamlet. An age in which the technology of services like Snapchat influences teenagers' sexual experiences and insurance companies offer policies to protect against cyberbullying.[1]

How well is society prepared for the consequences of being digitalized? What sort of educational concepts has it developed to teach citizens how to use new technologies in socially responsible ways? It may be amusing and astonishing to learn that in Germany the country's transportation minister hands out prizes for educational computer games and convenes an ethics commission to discuss artificial intelligence. But this curiosity is part of a much deeper problem within educational systems. The paradigm for how schools treat media literacy is controlling traffic and not, as it should be, preventing crime. This is a major issue and, as this essay will show, the police themselves are among the main suspects.

TRAFFIC SCHOOL

When you look at how schools teach students about media, you could easily get the idea that, both metaphorically and in terms of personnel, education on the subject is firmly in the hands of the police. Police run video campaigns about the dangers of texting on the streets and warn on their websites about phishing, scams, Trojan horses, ransomware, cyberbullying, and sexting. Officers regularly visit schools to inform the students about data security, the addictive potential of computer games, ways of avoiding explicit pornographic and violent content, and the legal ramifications of illegal downloads. Even when the topic is online criminality and police hand out pamphlets with titles like "Secure Use of the Internet, Mobile Phones and Computer Games: In the Network of New Media" as part of their crime-prevention efforts, the underlying educational model is that of traffic school. The goal is to teach people types of behavior so as to avoid accidents in the digital realm.[2]

Such seminars even come with certificates reminiscent of those you can get at traffic school. There are "licenses" to surf and use computers and new media. The progenitor of this sort of thing was the European Computer Driving License handed out since 1995 by the Council of European Professional Informatics Societies (CEPIS) for skill in using computer applications. Brochures about the advantages and risks of social media often have titles like "Buckling Up in Cyber-Space," an Austrian promotional campaign for including media skills as part of IT education was called "Media Education in the Passing Lane," and a standard work of German media pedagogy asserted "Soon we will all be driving down the data highway."[3]

The proper term for this approach is less media *education* than media *competence* since the knowledge imparted is the practical kind, of students knowing how to use things rationally to achieve specific ends instead of engaging in any theoretical or philosophical reflection. Theoretical or philosophical questions would include: How are new media changing society? What should we think about that change? As it stands, however, we merely ask ourselves: How can we use new media effectively and securely? To stay with the traffic metaphor, children are supposed to learn street smarts, and indeed many users of the data highway are just trying to get away with violating the "rules of the road," for instance by illegally downloading movies and music.[4]

The traffic model has history on its side. The Internet was introduced to the public at large in the Bill Clinton/Al Gore era as the "information superhighway," and twenty years before that, in 1974, the father of media arts Nam June Paik, who lived in Germany, called the telecommunications network of the future the "electronic super-Autobahn."[5] One of the bizarre results of viewing digital media from the perspective of highway systems is that the price of educational computer games in Germany is set by the transportation minister. This is not because he or she is an expert in computer games or pedagogy but because computer games are considered part of the country's "digital infrastructure," akin to the expansion of the broadband network or the allocation of broadcast frequencies. Thus they fall under that ministry's aegis.

Against this backdrop, it is hardly surprising that the German Ministry of Education and Research has traditionally considered media education to be an infrastructure issue, and its main priority has been to get schools connected to the web. In 1996, together with Deutsche Telekom, the ministry founded the *Schulen ans Netz* (Schools onto the Net) association to provide German schools with free access to the Internet.[6] The five billion euros that the ministry pledged in October 2016 to invest in broadband, WiFi, and hardware for 40,000 schools was also primarily directed at planning traffic—not in the sense of modern highways, but rather in terms of computers and educational methods as vehicles for "transporting knowledge." In the words of Germany's education minister, there was a "primacy of pedagogy,"[7] by which she meant what teachers consider to be sensible uses of digital media. But can we really expect the traffic model to give education the right of way over the interests of—the digital equivalent of the "car lobby"—the IT sector?

REVOLUTION FROM ABOVE

Whenever the digitalization of schools today is praised as an "educational revolution," what otherwise might simply be called an investment program leads us back to Australia, where in 2008 the government began to equip schools with the Internet and older students with laptops under the slogan "Digital Education Revolution." As in the case of many revolutions, this one was, at times, fairly hit-or-miss. It is doubtful that today we know any better than the French revolutionaries of 1789 did about where things are headed. What good is so much Internet in the classroom? Rarely have any attempts been made to calculate the future costs of such a pool of digital capabilities, nor are teachers necessarily convinced that such a revolution from above makes pedagogical sense. As the death of Georges Danton shows, it's often dangerous to criticize the revolution, even if you yourself are a revolutionary.

Today's revolutionaries argue that schools need to be closely tied to "real life" and that today's youth cannot be prepared for the future with the tools of the past. The accusation of anachronism is often accompanied by the phrase "the end of the chalk age." But just because they're pithy doesn't make slogans like this correct. Age is no more a disgrace than youth is a virtue—this is true of teaching materials as well. Those students who didn't fall asleep or get distracted by WhatsApp when their history instructor was trying to teach them about the Russian Revolution will be wary of assuming that everything new is always better. Moreover, anyone who takes any interest in the internal workings of the tech world and knows how many CEOs of IT companies enroll their children in technology-free Waldorf schools will ask him- or herself what sorts of risks to children their products entail that they're not telling their customers about.[8]

While the transition from the chalk to the digital age may represent progress, we can also see stages of education as stages of media history that all retain a certain validity. This perspective favors introducing young people to communicative media in the order that they arose historically. Under this logic, children should first learn to talk, sing, and paint, then to read and to take photographs, before they turn to electronic and digital media. But there are objections. Notwithstanding the fact that it would be hard to imitate the historical development of media on the individual level in an authentic environment, tech-savvy parents might argue that the computer is a multifaceted device and can be used as a book, a camera, a radio, and a TV so that kids might as well be introduced to it in kindergarten. However, even more tech-savvy parents will know that the computer also fundamentally changes all of these traditional media. The text on a computer screen is not the digital equivalent of a printed twin, but a fully new entity. The technological and social conditions of the new environment, which includes properties like interactivity, hyperlinking, and multitasking, and its culture of hyper-attention and hyper-stimulation radically contradict the culture of book reading that arose in the eighteenth century.

Actually, it's absurd to think that the more digital media determine life outside school, the more they should be included in education. Without doubt, as educational revolutionaries never tire of pointing out, one main task of schools is to help actively shape the future. But that doesn't mean the chalkboard has to be eliminated entirely in favor of the computer. The advent of modern transportation doesn't mean that people no longer walk anywhere farther away than the length of their car. On the contrary, it was precisely the advent of automotive society that made it necessary to restrict the dominance of the car by creating bicycle lanes, pedestrianized streets, and emissions standards for inner-city driving. Would it not be reasonable to try to reduce the amount of digital smog in schoolchildren's minds?

If schools conceive of themselves as places of conservation for both the human knowledge and human abilities developed over the course of history, then part of their task is to defend cultural techniques that are under threat. For example, the ability to read and write complex essays—to which digital media do not lend themselves. Or to listen attentively—this is certainly not among the cardinal virtues of Internet culture with its mania for participation, which encourages people to keep talking when they no longer have anything to say. So does that mean schools should be doing more frontal classroom instruction than group work, more reading and writing than browsing and posting?

It's hardly a sign of pedagogical vision if the custodian, as revolutionaries sometimes sneer, is the only one in school who knows how to turn on a computer. Teachers who automatically refuse to use digital media in their instruction are cheating their students and themselves out of valuable opportunities for learning. For instance, nothing speaks against using online forums and wikis to work on projects or sharing the results of one's work outside the protective space of the classroom, say, in the form of a blog or a Wikipedia entry. Why should a subject like English not profit from the Internet by allowing students to discuss literary texts with strangers on "social reading" platforms, to describe their own imaginative trips around the world in eight days on a blog, on Facebook, Instagram, Snapchat, or Twitter, and hence, through the use of these various social networks, to sensitize themselves to the communicative consequences of medial differences? What is there to criticize about computer animations of chemical reactions, three-dimensional immersion in the human body, or the reenactment of historical events on Twitter and Facebook? All of these examples and many other ways of using digital and social media in classrooms are completely sensible, both from a didactic and a pedagogical perspective, and should not be sacrificed to some teachers' fears of computers.[9]

HOSTAGE TAKING AND BRIBERY

But many teachers' skepticism about the revolution that is being forced upon them cannot be reduced to technological skittishness and refusal to innovate. Educators often have good didactic, pedagogical, and political reasons to be wary, particularly concerning assertions that distance learning, global teachers, online campuses, computer-based learning, and personal learning environments are the future of education. If the automatization and personalization of learning reduces learning to the level of grammar drills disguised as gamification, and if the solidarity created by group instruction falls victim to algorithm-driven self-optimization, education gets sacrificed to the ideas of software developers and IT companies. That is not a sensible continuation of existing educational reform initiatives with digital means.

It is by no means shocking that teachers' advocacy groups have been outspoken in criticizing the disempowerment of educational experts by specialists from outside the educational system. The chairperson of the Association of German Teachers, for example, dismissed the "digital pact" offered by the education ministry as a "stimulus package for the computer industry," which would have the "collateral damage" of reducing students' concentration abilities by increasing their dependency on computers and would allow search engines to diminish knowledge into bite-sized snippets. In much the same sense, the nonprofit group Lobby-Control accuses IT companies of trying to force Apple laptops, "Google for Education," or Microsoft partnerships for improving IT equipment into schools, and of misusing those schools as sites for acquiring customers and teaching them how to use their products.[10]

The notion that the Ministry of Education may be sacrificing its own area of responsibility to benefit commercial interests may seem exaggerated, but it's hardly reassuring that Germany's Federal Association for IT, Telecommunications and New Media (Bitkom) responded to the criticism from teachers' organizations by saying that 80 percent of parents surveyed indicated their support for more investment in digital teaching aids and "a broader treatment of digital topics in instruction." The conditions under which this survey was carried out remain secret. But the list of the digital topics desired clearly reflected the traffic school model:

data protection and the legal basics of the Internet, proper behavior in chatrooms and on social media, the use of apps and programs, and career opportunities in the digital economy. It's understandable that parents have no objections to schools educating their kids about topics like these. But why did Bitkom's survey exclusively ask parents about topics related to practical, action-oriented knowledge and not those concerning theoretical or philosophical reflection?[11]

The support of this IT-industry lobbying organization for the digital education revolution is easy to understand. Business has an interest in seeing society digitalized as quickly as possible, and nowhere is this interest more evident than in the keynote speech Bitkom president Thorsten Dirks delivered at Germany's Digital-Gipfel summit in June 2017. Dirks demanded that German think in terms of "digital first" with "maximum tempo," "no ifs, ands or buts." His speech often sounded like an invitation to gamble with no regard to the consequences, secure in the knowledge that the rest of society would pick up the pieces. "We can't afford to get lost in the details now," Dirks told his audience. "We need to bet everything on a single card, the digital one."[12] Five months earlier, at the Bitkom conference Bildung 4.0, Germany's Education Minister Johanna Wanka translated the Bitkom president's enthusiastic slogans for Industry 4.0 into the language of educational policy: "Digital technologies come on the market with tremendous speed, and that means we have to be constantly prepared to accept novelties and learn new things. Anyone who enlists the aid of digital technology must learn to steer it, whether in the workplace or in private life. You need the ability to evaluate."[13] It was no accident that Wanka talked about evaluating specific situations and not generally reflecting on the bigger picture. To keep with the traffic metaphor: the point is to drive defensively, not to question the rules of the road.

What is so remarkable about Wanka's programmatic statement is not the Ministry of Education's ease in cooperating with business interests—the ministry's reorientation away from the neohumanistic concept of universal education and toward a scholastically humanist concept of training in line with the market's needs did not start with the 1999 Bologna Process. The reduction of education to communication of the skills needed by a digitally dominated society and digitally oriented labor market is the logical extension of its commercialization. Educational and research policy is subordinated to economic policy, which is often criticized as focusing on *Homo economicus* instead of *Zoon politikon*. Whereas the latter understood him- or herself as a part of the common body politic, responsible for that community, the former is concerned first and foremost with enhancing his or her portfolio value in all domains of life. It is this social context that explains the educational system's reduction of media competence to the knowledge necessary to adequately serve the market.[14]

What is far more remarkable is that the former German Economics Minister Sigmar Gabriel himself complained about the educational focus on instrumental rather than reflective media competence. In his opening speech at the German national IT summit in November 2016, Gabriel stressed the need for education to achieve both skills and orientation: "Orientation in a changing world is the precondition for remaining autonomous ... and capable of emancipation. That's why digitalization is about more than acquiring technical skills and skills as users." People needed to know not just how to program or employ algorithms, Gabriel explained, but also what effects they can have on society and when they shouldn't be used. The question of the social consequences of algorithms demands that we shift the focus from instrumental media skills to reflection about media, from a traffic-based to a criminal investigative model of media educations.[15]

INTERNET AND THE HOMICIDE SQUAD

In a 2017 episode of the popular German crime show *Tatort*, the murder victim is a prankster whose death is followed by thousands of fans on their mobile phones, and a major theme is the helplessness of many parents in the face of their children's Internet culture. Representing, in a sense, overwhelmed mothers and fathers everywhere, Directing Police Commissioner Schnabel exclaims: "Can someone please turn off this goddamn Internet?" As absurd as that question may be, it underscores what's at stake in human interactions with technology. Whom does the Internet belong to? The obvious answer is that it belongs to the young people in the episode as well as to the commissioner, who also engages in online dating. But that fails to tell the whole story. The question of power is one not between human beings but rather between human beings and technology itself. In academic debates about the media we often phrase it as: do people control technology or vice versa? — *the question*

The optimistic answer is that technology, media, and tools are morally neutral. It's up to users whether new media are employed to write hateful tirades or love stories, whether a knife is used to slice a filet of pork or a fellow human being. It's more difficult to argue for the freedom of human will vis-à-vis technology, if we change weapons and try to argue that a pistol can be used to hammer nails just as a hammer can be used to bash in human skulls. While it's not impossible to use a pistol in this way, it is very unlikely. Certain types of technology entail certain usages, and psychologists and police statisticians agree that the presence of a pistol dramatically reduces the likelihood that a quarrel will end in reconciliation or mere verbal violence.

But statistics aren't the only arguments against the optimistic conviction that human beings are the sovereign masters over their use of technology. Media have their own messages, agendas that they force upon people, often without them even realizing or being able to resist. Human beings may be the ones who create media, but that doesn't mean that human beings can resist either the media's conditions for or possibilities of use, which the inventors may never have originally envisioned. A good example of this is the commissioner's use of online dating—as anyone knows who is still trying to find a suitable partner in a bar and not on the Internet.

Another example is provided by a second episode of *Tatort* from 2016, which features a set of contact lenses with a built-in camera that takes pictures and saves them to the cloud when the wearer is excited or agitated by what he or she is experiencing. That may sound spooky, but one day when contact lenses like these come on the market, they'll be sure to sell. Human beings under threat from the autonomous life of artificial intelligence, on which they so diligently and so successfully work, is a venerable literary and cinematic trope, as shown by two further *Tatort* episodes entitled "Echolot" (October 30, 2016) and "HAL" (August 28, 2016). In both cases, a computer program turns against its creators after the humans, fearing unforeseen consequences, sought to turn it off, and both cases result in a human death.

This brief overview of recent German crime drama illustrates what we can learn from watching shows like *Tatort*. You only have to pick up on the questions raised by the fictional police commissioners, and you're already deeply involved in an extremely complex discussion, beyond basic issues like how to open an app, create a website, or recognize fake news. Teachers could address the philosophical issue about the power of technology by asking: do you control your mobile phone or does it control you? Students might shoot back that it's possible to withdraw from the postulates of the media in question and treat a WhatsApp message like a letter instead of immediately dashing off a brief response, or write an extensive commentary of a Facebook update instead of merely liking it. But they would also very likely point out that doing so would be as strange as hammering a nail into the wall with a pistol.

Somewhat more complex but equally relevant to students' and teachers' actual experiences is the question of whether digital and social media not only allow fake news and hate speech but, thanks to the conditions of communicating in these media, actually encourage them. Yet no matter which questions are debated and how, anyone who understands that media create culture knows that they cannot be seen merely as information technologies and treated as a part of human traffic and infrastructure. The extension of this insight is that school teachers can be successful on this score only if they act like criminal investigators and not like traffic cops.

IMMIGRANT POLICE

It is no secret that the new media have not made relations between teachers and students any easier. How should a teacher treat a student who's become a star with half a million views per week in YouTube's beauty community? While the teacher is attempting to explain to her class the conflicts and contradictions of human life using literary examples, the student is changing the marketing strategies of the cosmetics industry. While the teacher is talking about some guy called Hamlet, the student is thinking about which other YouTube star she should invite to be on her show next week. While the teacher is assigning homework, the student is texting Nicoletta, who had a sex-change operation six months ago and is totally hot on the scene right now.

Things get even worse when teachers try to explain the Internet to their students. Even if instructors have only just graduated university and are themselves digital natives, they're still hopelessly out of date. The teachers too may use Facebook and Google, but are they up on all the latest apps? Have they heard of 4chan's Pepe? Do they know who Nicoletta is? It's a tortoise-and-hare race that the tortoises—the teachers—have no hope of winning. Some student is always already at the point where the teachers are trying to catch up to. In the traffic-based model of instruction, there's no way the teachers can be equal to their students' demands. This model may be justified in younger classes, and its metaphors can be didactically useful, as for instance is the *Medienkompass 1* of the Swiss intercantonal Center for Educational Materials,[16] which not only compares the Internet with street traffic, but also emails with taxis and links with the doors to houses youngsters should only knock on if they know who lives there. But in upper grades, it's often better to leave the teaching of know-how up to peer education, making the students themselves responsible for passing on knowledge.

At the same time, we should stop constantly giving teachers a false sense of inadequacy, as was the case at Germany's 2016 National IT Summit, when the chairwoman of the Conference of Culture Ministers declared that teachers shouldn't be ashamed if their students sometimes knew more than they did. The applause the audience gave to this remark signaled a kind of entirely wrongheaded understanding. The same was true of German Chancellor Angela

Merkel, who at the same event compared the respective media knowledge of teachers and students today with the early 1990s, when East Germans had to accept being told by much younger West Germans about all the things the former *didn't* know. Merkel's historical comparison between "digital immigrants" and East Germans "immigration" to West German society may have rung true, but Merkel didn't go as far as she could have. East Germans were not merely clueless about the system in the West; they also maintained more critical distance from this new social structure. People who have to consciously learn a political, linguistic, or media system instead of growing up with it reflect on it more. This is not a disadvantage for which the "poor teachers" require understanding, but an advantage that should be clearly identified as such.[17]

If teachers want to explain the Internet to their students, their only chance is to act like immigrants and detectives. Like immigrants, they must approach their new environment with the distance and skepticism of people who can draw comparisons with an earlier time and who know, for instance, what will be lost if hypertexts replace books. Like detectives, they must ask, when confronted with the suspicious activities of digital mavens and their innovation-producing startups, whether a crime has been committed and who can be arrested on what charges. In the *Tatort* episodes cited above, the detectives start out at a loss. Pranks are usually harmless, and it would be absurd to try to prosecute the producer of fake snuff videos for swindling the audience. Internet platforms for prostitution are no more or less legitimate than red-light districts. And in general, society considers the development of artificial intelligence and memory aids to be a sign of progress, not a crime.

No matter what answers the television detectives find to their questions, their uncertainty can be a useful pedagogical tool for teachers. Simplistic and naïve as these questions may be, skilled teachers can unlock their political import and philosophical depth in the classroom. A good point of departure could even be the absolutely ridiculous call to "turn off" the Internet.

TV COPS AND TEACHERS

At the start of the episode entitled "HAL," a girl wanders along a path through the woods whistling the old children's song "Hänschen klein" (Little Hans), when she sees a body in a river and throws a stick at it. The stick transforms itself midflight into a target, at which the episode's main character, a hipster, takes aim at a shooting club. Movie buffs will immediately recognize the reference to the famous early scene from Stanley Kubrick's *2001* in which the bone tossed in the air metamorphoses into the spaceship run by the computer HAL, who rebels against the astronauts and ends up, in the dubbed German version of the film, singing "Hänschen klein" when it is deactivated. (In the original, HAL sings "Daisy Bell.") In the episode of *Tatort*, a computer will also whistle "Hänschen klein"—but in this instance only after it has brought an entire system under its control.

The reason that these two songs were chosen is relatively banal. They were the first two pieces of music in history intoned and sung by computers: "Little Hans" by the Zuse 22 in Germany in 1958 and "Daisy Bell" by the IBM 704 in America in 1961. With "Hänschen klein," it's impossible to overlook the symbolism of HAL and "HAL"—an example of humans experimenting with artificial intelligence—singing a song about a child going out to explore the great wide world. The song, however, is an ambivalent symbol. In their original form, the lyrics describe Hänschen's emancipation from his family home, while in the more popular abridged version, they suggest that the child quickly breaks off his adventure and returns home to his weeping mother. In classroom instruction, we might ask: What does it mean that a rebellious computer starts singing this song at the very moment its power becomes complete? What is the relationship between this scenario and the singing of the same song in a diametrically opposite situation in Kubrick's film? Which version of the song is meant in both instances?[18]

Classroom discussions in the course of a philosophically oriented media education will by necessity reflect the genre of this musical Bildungsroman. "Little Hans" has to grow up to be adult Hans—that's the law of development that governs not only the individual but the whole species. Those who stay at home may avoid all the dangers the world holds in store, including getting caught out in the rain or being killed by a loose roof tile, but they will never be able to make tomorrow different from today. Humanity's fate is not stasis, but innovation, which leads humans to constantly

innovation

change their environment and which is sometimes called progress, sometimes destruction. Cultural paradigms are also altered by this process and by things like artificial intelligence and memory-possessing contact lenses. There is more than enough material for further classroom instruction. Questions for discussion could include: to what extent do technological innovations "export revolution" into other, more statically organized cultures; how successfully can society regulate technological progress; and is society capable of turning off disagreeable aspects of the Internet, be it via laws to sanction fake news and hate speech on social media, as is the case controversially right now in Germany, or by banning undesired experiments, as is the case in genetic technology and reproductive medicine?

We might formulate a question for a homework assignment as follows: which laws would you propose to allow the television detectives to combat this or that IT startup? To hone students' reflective capacities in the sense of media history, we might challenge them to define the difference between contemporary technology innovations and earlier ones, such as the replacement of the horse-drawn carriage by the automobile or home-made music by the gramophone. Or we could concentrate on bits of dialogue from the *Tatort* episodes that run through various individual reactions to technological innovations and reflect divisions in society that also exist in the classroom.[19]

Discussing the philosophical implications of technological progress using a children's song and a TV crime show may not be part of the typical syllabus. But things like this could offer a way forward to teachers who refuse to let themselves by cowed by the greater knowledge of their "digital native" students and are creative enough to discuss new media using old texts, be it "Hänschen klein" or Kafka's *Metamorphosis* or *The Trial*, both of which crop up in the "HAL" episode as intertitles. Shelly's *Frankenstein* (1818) and Goethe's ballad *The Sorcerer's Apprentice* (1797) are two other classical literary works dealing with artificial intelligence turning against its creators.

To initiate this discussion, it's not even necessary to train teachers in media theory in any systematic way. All that's required to start is a familiarity with crime shows like *Tatort* and other comparable products of pop culture, the corresponding pedagogical interest, a didactic inspiration for getting students to talk about such topics, an inquisitiveness about details such as why a children's song should occur in a crime show episode about AI, and the ability to use technology to explain the origin of such details—that is, the basic skill of using a search engine.[20]

This brief look at German crime shows illustrates not just the divergent stature of the questions that arise from a criminal-investigative approach to new media. It also suggests the different results we get when we view media education like a detective and not like a traffic cop. The teacher as traffic cop might perhaps try to enliven lessons on Goethe's ballad, which is about summoning spirits that can no longer be controlled, with computer animation, in essence using the latest technology to avoid talking *about* technology. The teacher as detective, on the other hand,

— detector vs tratore cup

even without the help of computers, would use technology as a bridge between Goethe and *Tatort* and back again, examining questions like: which spirits are we actually conjuring up, and which ones would we like to get rid of again?

THE SURVEILLANCE STATE AND SELF-ACCUSATION

The detectives in *Tatort* of course don't speak in the name of the police, but in the name of art or, to be more accurate, in the name of a culture industry more critical than Adorno led us to believe and the police themselves would probably like. TV detectives who raise our awareness of potentially dangerous media development are not only social irritants. Their own colleagues are also in their line of fire. In "HAL," it turns out that the state criminal police are secretly using the artificial intelligence developed by the startup in their fight against terrorism and are thus laying the groundwork for the total surveillance of the population.

This denouement is no huge surprise. In episodes from other series, for example, "Hated in the Nation" from Britain's *Black Mirror*, self-steering drone insects (i.e., tiny robots equipped with cameras) not only take over the pollination work of bees, which have gone extinct, but also help intelligence services keep track of people by means of facial recognition software. The ongoing debates about data preservation and "predictive policing" have left no doubt that police see digital media as valuable tools and allies allowing them to do the jobs society has tasked them with more efficiently.

This is certainly true of traffic police, who have welcomed the increasing interconnectedness of cars, which allows them to communicate with one another and hopefully decrease accidents at intersections and on highways. Additionally the on-board computer is a model driver who strictly follows speed limits and right-of-way rules. Police are looking forward to backward-facing cameras in cars that record not the flow of traffic for use in trials but the faces of drivers to recognize the warning signs of overexertion that can cause crashes. Many officers also dream of remote control over the vehicles used by recidivist speed demons or criminals on the lam, who can be brought to a halt without any car chases or roadblocks. The fact that the police will tend to leave security gaps in such systems open so that they can use them means that organized crime, too, will exploit them, sooner or later, to spread ransomware. This illustrates how inadvertently criminal the behavior of the police can be.[21]

In bringing nightmare visions of total police monitoring into German living rooms, the TV detectives of *Tatort* function not as colleagues, but adversaries of the real police. In a sense they are civil rights activists in uniform. Media literacy that, like the fictional detectives, problematizes the social effects of technological developments is desirable only insofar as it is still the job of education to turn students into critical citizens. We will examine shortly whether this is still the case. For now, it's sufficient to point out the violations by the police themselves, whose unprofessional use of digital media calls forth critical reflection on how police use these technologies.

In July 2017, a number of legitimate journalists saw their accreditation revoked for the G20 Summit in Hamburg. A subsequent investigation revealed that a series of technical mistakes had been made with the reporters' data: confusion with names, a lack of skepticism toward sources, and ideological blunders such as classifying opponents of nuclear power as people trying to topple the German economy and government. In the end, no one knew why certain people were flagged as potential security risks, but that didn't change the fact that these people were wrongly denied access to such a major event. The German police would never allow a motor vehicle in as poor a shape as their own databases even to take the road.

The mistakes made in the context of G20 were seen as a wake-up call about the inherent dangers of getting carried away with surveillance data, although some speculated that politicians tacitly approved of the excesses.[22] If we want to engage in a bit of conspiracy theorizing, we might ask: Is it possible that the traffic-based model of media educations is a diversion intended to suppress the sorts of critical questions raised by the *Tatort* detectives from the public's mind? Does the way media literacy is conceived in German schools aim to produce vigilant drivers but not vigilant citizens?

POLITICAL RIGHT OF WAY

We have good reason to distrust the political treatment of artificial intelligence that was flagged as so dangerous in the *Tatort* episode. As is the case with prizes for pedagogically valuable computer games, it's rather astonishing that debates in Germany about AI are conducted by the Ministry of Transport and Digital Infrastructure and not the Ministry of the Interior or Justice. Still, this situation is somewhat comprehensible insofar as AI behind the wheels of self-driving cars will soon be a force to be reckoned on the real-life Autobahn, and not just the information superhighway. It was entirely legitimate for the transportation minister to convene an ethics commission in early 2016 to consider the implications of self-driving cars. What's problematic—and what occasions mistrust—is the role given to such a commission in political planning.

In their final report, issued in June 2017, the commission concluded that the complete networking of traffic carried the danger of total surveillance and an encroachment upon the protection of individuals' data. This showed the commission members were aware of the problem. This body recognized that the attempt to use technology to further good ends—preventing motorists from driving aggressively and violating speed limits—"contradicted the ideal of the responsible, sovereign citizen" and thus "ran contrary to the basis of a humane, free society." This conclusion makes it clear that the question of self-driving cars should not be the sole responsibility of the transportation minister. The self-driven car may well turn out to be a Trojan horse with which limitations on individual freedoms are justified in the interests of the "efficiency-based digital infrastructure" and "an increase in traffic comfort and safety." To quote the report itself again: "self-driving cars would come at the cost of self-determination in everyday actions."[23] In that case, the

Ministry of Transport and Digital Infrastructure would serve as a vehicle for social regression.

Equally unsettling was the commission's statement that the "systemic instability," the possibility that the digital control of traffic might get hacked, was an "acceptable utilitarian risk," as long as that possibility was considered to be remote. How can we calculate "the acceptable risks of an instance of abuse of such central power structures"? How many manipulated crashes would it take for us to pull the plug on digitalizing traffic? A hundred? A thousand? And what is the decisive criterion, the number of accidents, of injuries or, of fatalities?[24]

It's hard to take the ethics commission to task for not be able to clear up these issues. Questions this important require much more extended debate in both a philosophical and technological sense. They exemplify the fact that technological breakthroughs praised as "disruptive innovations" in the jargon of revolution cannot be put into practice in society with the sort of rapidity that companies and economists would like. The question we are facing as a society is whether we can afford or ever want to take the time to discuss such ethical problems comprehensively and, in the best case, democratically—or whether the politicians give the economy right of way before morality.

In the case at hand, the latter has proven to be the case. The German minister of transport greenlighted the development of self-driving cars before the ethics commission had even published its final report. The convening of the commission seems to have been a symbolic fig leaf that merely helped the state to justify the pursuit of what it had wanted all along. No matter what the ethics specialists concluded, the self-driving car had to be developed—it would be a catastrophe if the exaggerated concerns of data protection advocates and technology skeptics caused the German automotive industry to lose market share to its rivals. On the grand political stage, there are ways to get things through inspection that aren't completely safe, and it's all the easier the fewer vigilant citizens there are asking undesired questions.

The *Tatort* episode "Echolot" warns against such a cavalier approach to the social consequences of the new media, whose risks are apparent even to the traffic-cop mentality. The episode is about the manipulation of data concerning a deadly accident, and its creators' awareness of the problems related to this issue is obviously far greater than that of the transport minister's ethics commission. In the episode, the accident is caused not by a hacker, but by an artificial intelligence itself that decides to do away with a person who, on moral grounds, wants to shut it down. Since this person was the same one who created the computer program in the first place, the interesting criminalist question arises: Who should be arrested? The software? The victim? And what is the basis for a prosecution? Was it murder or self-defense? Or a new, highly symbolic form of suicide consisting of the creation of uncontrollable programs, which are then left unattended and irregularly maintained?

Those who dismiss such scenarios as mere fiction don't recognize how serious the situation truly is, especially when we consider that the criminal energy of hackers could also mean disaster. The question is not how realistic the episode entitled "Broken Hearts" from the series *Homeland* was when it depicted a death caused by a pacemaker being hacked. The question is whether the hacking of hospitals in the United States and Germany in 2016 and in Britain in 2017 (by the WannaCry worm), as well as all the other, less famous hacks of industrial facilities and state institutions, are harbingers of a future in which criminals hold citizens hostage because the politicians have allowed the Internet of things to be built without the necessary foresight and with no enforcement of up-to-date security standards. Will the approval of behind-the-wheel software by what the transport minister praises as "the most modern traffic legal system in the world" mean that we'll all be driving around with ransomware in our transmission and be forced to pay regular protection money like shop owners in a mafia-controlled neighborhood? Will we be confined to house arrest until the ransom is paid or until someone repairs the bug that prevents us from opening the "smart doors" of our own homes?[25]

DIGITAL DRIVERS

In view of many ongoing debates about education, the assertion that the state prefers attentive participants in traffic over vigilant citizens looks less like a conspiracy theory than it is meant to be. Critics of the Swiss initiative Lehrplan 21 talk of "state-ordered political helplessness" that will produce "ideological warriors for a cost-cutting ideology of subservience." Observers in Germany describe the neoliberalization and commercialization of the country's school system as the reduction of "education to competence ... [and] attitudes to good behavior." This, say the German critics, entails the loss of "the autonomous capacity for critique and judgement, which according to Humboldt's theory of state are both the precondition and consequence of freedom." In the United States, philosophers Martha Nussbaum and Wendy Brown lambast the American educational system as producing "useful machines, rather than complete citizens who can think for themselves" and warn against failing to view the liberal arts as "binding, developing, or renewing us as a people, alerting us to dangers, or providing frames, figures, theories, and allegories ... [and] providing the various capacities required for democratic citizenship."[26]

Regardless of how justified these criticisms may or may not be, they are also examples of worries that the long-term investment in a democratic society will take a back seat to short-term economic interests. And such worries are hardly assuaged by the fact that when "digital citizenship" is taught, it aims primarily at inculcating practical skills: the ability to multitask and communicate in various modes, to network, collaborate, navigate, find information, and evaluate results, as well as, in response to fake news and hate speech, the ability to critique sources, evaluate quality, maintain netiquette, and avoid cyberbullying and trolling. This sort of digital citizenship does not aim to encourage critical reflection upon people's social environment, including its social media aspects. On the contrary, as the terms above suggest, it tries to get students to learn the "traffic rules" so that they have a frictionless, positive experience of online interactions. The Cyberwise organization, for example, writes: "Just like Driver's Education prepares young people to get behind the wheel of a car, Digital Citizenship prepares them to navigate the Information Superhighway safely and confidently."[27]

Here it must be stressed again that there is nothing wrong with teaching students such "traffic skills"—unless of course they are put forward as all anyone needs to know in order to act as a responsible citizen in the age of digital media. As Brown argues, it would be a fatal mistake to conceive democracy "as requiring technically skilled human capital, not educated participants in public life and common rule." And as Brown continues, it would be a fatal mistake to reduce education to rendering people operational for the labor market. If digital-citizenship curricula in schools is limited to the teaching of technical abilities, of producing "productive and responsible users of digital technologies," we are not just coming up short. We degrade the concept of the citizen as a symbolic representative of a political responsibility that goes beyond immediate personal interests. This is precisely the attack on democracy that emerges if we examine the politics of media education.[28]

TYPES OF CITIZENSHIP

Brown's and Nussbaum's criticism of the neoliberal remaking of educational systems echoes the warnings about economically oriented understanding of democracy issued by

Canadian philosopher and political scientist Charles Taylor a quarter-century ago. In his essay "Some Conditions of a Viable Democracy," Taylor described a model of democracy whose central idea was that of "political society as a common instrument set up to further the purposes of the individuals who constitute it." The basic unit of calculation of what Taylor called the "economic theory" of democracy is the individual, whose aims and wishes demanded to be prioritized as frequently as possible. Should that not be the case, the political leadership will be voted out in the next election, in the same way that consumers change service providers if they are dissatisfied with the product on offer. For Taylor, this sort of consumer behavior is deeply problematic: "What this model leaves out, of course, is what has always been considered the virtues and dignity of citizenship, that people take an active part in their own government, that they in some sense rule themselves."[29]

Taylor argues as a Hegelian. Just as Hegel subordinated the individual to the "moral state" as a "substantial unit" and the "highest duty," Taylor orients the individual toward a community that serves as the absolute linchpin of a functioning democracy. That may at first seem alienating, as history has shown the problematic consequences of an emphatic concept of a normative community of values. But if we understand Taylor's promotion of "patriotism" in terms of cosmopolitanism and state constitutions, it is indisputable that democracy depends on citizens feeling themselves "bound very particularly to their compatriots in a common defense of these rights." By contrast, the economic model of democracy, which Taylor calls "parasitic," reflects the corrupting of consumer culture that "present-day capitalism" brings with it. On the one hand, this aspect of capitalism—Taylor is specifically referring to large international corporations—is "effectively draining the power of participatory institutions, and transferring it to irresponsible bureaucratic organizations." On the other hand, "the whole ideology of consumerism it supports tends to induce us to acquiesce in this abdication of responsibility, in return for the promised continuing rise in individual living standards." As a result of this development—and twenty-five years on, it may make us think of the successful model of depoliticization in Chinese state capitalism—popular political participation "seems rather a menace to the smooth running of the system; and democracy as the common repository of citizen dignity is in danger."[30]

Taylor addresses a problem of postmodern, postdemocratic, and postnational societies in which people no longer feel part of a community. The fact that this proceeds hand in hand with a turn away from ideology and politics was registered a few years after Taylor's essay by John Katz, who described the birth of the "digital nation" as "libertarian, materialist, tolerant" but also "postpolitical." The citizens of this nation are meritocratic individualists who don't want anyone to tell them how to live but also don't feel responsible for how anyone else lives either. The article describes the difference in terms of a familiar metaphor: "If liberals say, 'Here's the tent: we have to get everyone inside,' and conservatives say, 'Here's the tent: we don't want it to get

the postpolitical

too crowded inside,' the postpolitical young say, 'Here's the tent: everyone is welcome—but everyone has to figure out how to get inside on his or her own.'"[31]

The intellectual foundation of this new nation was quickly dismissed as a "Californian ideology" that "promiscuously combines the free-wheeling spirit of the hippies and the entrepreneurial zeal of the yuppies." This was a dotcom take on neoliberalism, which as a form of "reactionary modernism" divorced economic progress from social progress. While there was a lot of emphasis in this ideology on the Internet as an electronic agora and marketplace that would strengthen democratic rights and social security, even twenty years ago, it was clear this was a case of the new "virtual class" kidding itself. The enthusiasm at the prospect of the Internet making the world more democratic is long gone. All that remains is the "postpolitical," "parasitic" citizen as a phenomenon of our times.[32]

DIALECTIC OF EGOTISM

Thinking about the economic model of democracy and the California ideology sensitizes us toward certain processes in the context of media education. If digital citizenship is mostly about teaching students how to use digital media safely and effectively and not to critically reflect on the consequences they have on society and human solidarity, it is an example of the transition from *Homo politicus* to *Homo economicus* and an accompanying semantic kidnapping. The politically and philosophically rich concept of the citizen is reduced to the knowledge possessed by a competent participant in traffic, capable of hyper-attention and multi-tasking, well-versed in netiquette, and able to circumnavi-gate fake information, pernicious friendship requests, and troll attacks. This sort of citizenship is not guided by a concern for society but for how individuals can make their way in it.

The focus of media education on the individual ego reflects the utilitarianism of the promoters of the digital educational revolution over and against education in the classic humanist sense. The starting point is the popular adage: learn not for school but for life. As proponents of neoliberal education write: "Classroom material or topics without any 'why' or 'why should I' leads to schools and uni-versities that are only about cramming."[33] Insofar as the "why question" centers on the career implications or practi-cal relevance of a subject, it follows the logic of *Homo eco-nomicus*, who isn't interested in education for its own sake. Orienting education around direct individual interests may seem sensible in the context of the economic model of democracy, which is also focused on individual interest— but this is only the case, if we overlook the dialectic of egotism.

The most efficient way to keep individuals down is to separate them from the group. This is one of the ABCs of all trade unions, who know that individual interests can be best advanced collectively. Ultimately, no matter how cool the millennials with their one-person startup may consider themselves, the emphasis on individualism does nothing but condition people to conform. Adaptation is a phenomenon of neoliberalism, in which everyone competes pitilessly against everyone else in life. Ironically, the dialectic of egotism articulates itself even when individuals become politically active—one example being the current obsessive focus on the politics of individual identity, which clearly hinders the formation of group-specific interests.[34]

As far as the new media are concerned, the dialectic of self-deception became the ironic slogan of 2016 congress of the Chaos Computer Club: "Works for me." The implication was that new media didn't work perfectly for either individuals or businesses, as shown by hack attacks, uncontrolled data commerce, and other phenomena. The CCC issued a clear warning: questions and problems concerning new media from security to reliability to values can only be solved collectively. The question thus should be: does it work for us?

This shift from the first-person singular to the first-person plural lies at the very heart of media literacy. The common question of how *I* can use new media efficiently and safely cuts off any examination of how new media change *our* situation as human beings. But precisely this sort of investigation, which is not about the traffic rules but about the meaning behind them, expresses itself in our feelings of citizenship, in the preservation of what Taylor sees as the basis for a stable democracy. It is the transition from literacy in the sense of how to use media competently, to literacy in the sense of how to reflect critically upon them, taking us from a traffic-cop to a detective model of media education.

THE TRUE SIXTH SENSE

In 2017, the Swiss city of Zug hosted a symposium on education and school directions with the title "Education 5.0? The Future of Learning—The Future of School" that focused on what current education processes aim to achieve. If Education 4.0 was oriented around "learning and education processes in an age of digital change," the introduction to the symposium proposed that Education 5.0 would have to consider "a stronger emphasis on personality development, basic values, empowerment, democracy and collective responsibility."[35] If we combine these ideas from 2017 with Taylor's propositions from 1993, it's not difficult to draw certain conclusions about media education.

Media education is an arena in which the battles of the future will be fought, all the more so as education seems to have lost its political function. As places of exo-socialization, schools and universities were traditionally places in which people were conditioned to become citizens. For a long time, all over the world, the goal of education was to install a sense of national consciousness. In the Federal Republic of Germany, historical experience demanded that education be above all about producing independently thinking citizens who supported and promoted the preservation and betterment of democracy. This interest was characterized by the conviction that individual people could profit from democracy only if it was ensured that everyone could do this. The mindset that wanted to educate people into independently thinking citizens was thus aware of the dialectic of selfishness and the common welfare.

In today's schools and universities, this consciousness of the importance of citizenship has to compete for attention with the neoliberal, egoist sense of self. In the case of media education, this expresses itself not only in the personal pronouns we choose to formulate our questions, but also in different sorts of subject matters. Whereas, in the interests of bettering comparison of individuals' competitive positions, neoliberalism uses social media ranking and reduces the stance of resistance to the ability to thwart CCTV surveillance cameras, political and philosophical citizenship problematizes the effects of surveillance and ranking on society as a whole. Whereas the neoliberal ego wants to know how he or she can rent out his or her apartment most profitably on Airbnb, citizens want to know to what extent Airbnb, Uber, and other platform capitalists create precarious labor conditions and threaten social harmony. Citizens ask not how to protect contact lenses with built-in cameras from being hacked but rather what consequences this technology will have for our memories. Citizens ask not how algorithms can be used more efficiently to classify individual interests and needs, but rather about the future costs of such classification.

Whereas the neoliberal approach defines digital citizenship as fluency in the rules of traffic, the political-philosophical approach defines it, in part, as reflection on the consequences of new technologies, including their effects on the formation of political convictions and on the labor market. This model of media education is, in the deeper sense, "part of political education and contributes to the development of our freedom-, justice- and solidari-ty-oriented society"[36]—words used by the highest education authority in Germany itself. The citizenship model of media education asks questions about the tacit message of the media. It develops people's sense about the dangers lurking within the new media as a detective, not a traffic cop, does. It is this interest, and not the drive to digitalize our educational methods by any means, that should primarily inspire our efforts to combine media and education.

5 CANNIBALISM AND NEW MEDIA

The idea of one person eating another often serves as an explanatory model for cultural phenomena in modern times, as is exemplified by bell hooks's 1992 essay on partnership, entitled "Eating the Other." hooks's subject is not the usual metaphors applying to lovers who "simply devour one another." Instead she's interested in racist "snacking." In "cross-racial dating," hooks contends, white men seek adventures with black women to add the spice of an exotic experience to their middle-class futures with white women. The Other, which hooks defines as the foreign ethnicity and culture of the partner in this experience, never becomes a fixed part of the men's lives. On the contrary, the women are merely tried out and come with an inherent sell-by date. The Other is consumed and forgotten. Such snacking is racist precisely because it never progresses beyond snacking.[1]

A decade later, Lisa Nakamura applied this sort of metaphoric cannibalism to the Internet. This time, the subject matter was role playing with identities in cyberspace, specifically white males using female, Asian avatars with handles like Miss_Saigon and Geisha_Guest. Nakamura considers this form of dressing up and making believe with a foreign ethnic identity a form of "empty tourism," which doesn't enrich the role-player in any way. It is symbolic appropriation of another's ethnic identity that is tried out for fun and without any consequences.[2]

hooks and Nakamura use cannibalism as a shorthand metaphor with pejorative connotations. But back in 1928, the Brazilian modernist writer Oswald de Andrade elevated it into a cultural creed in his *Manifesto Antropófago (Anthropophagic Manifesto)*. By anthropophagy, he meant a ritualistic cannibalism which he promoted as a way of finding Brazilian identity. Brazilians, de Andrade argued, should neither ignore nor submit to European cultural influences. They should accept, internalize, and digest them with irony, parody, and disrespect.

If we apply the cultural and philosophical idea of cannibalism at work in all three of these cases through the lens of media theory, we can identify various digital media phenomena as forms of "transmedial cannibalism." Here the Other is the venerable medium of written text, whose symbolic consumption takes place as it is transformed into a postliterate object and a "musicalized" event.

RAINING LETTERS

One early example of this constellation is Romy Achituv and Camille Utterback's interactive installation *Text Rain* from 1999. Individual letters descend slowly from the entire upper surface of a projection screen, and when observers approach the screen they see their own image recorded and projected by a hidden camera in the middle. The installation is programmed so that the letters stop falling when they meet a darker section of screen. That allows observers to use their own bodies to collect, pick up, drop, and catch the letters again.

The installation was particularly successful because it allowed observers to encounter text in such a special way. Suddenly, letters were no longer linguistic bearers of meaning that needed to be decoded, although that was in fact possible since the letters were taken from a poem and formed words and lines, if observers were patient enough to collect them. But of course hardly anyone thought of putting the letters together and reading them when they could be scooped up with an umbrella and balanced on fingertips. Experience showed that the audience didn't pay much attention to the text in *Text Rain*.

Another example is *Bit.Fall* by Julius Popp from 2006. In this roughly two-meter high and five-meter wide installation, hundreds of valves released drops of water so that they formed letters. Meanwhile, horizontally, the letters formed words. The words were taken from Internet announcements of world events and had a visual life of only two or three seconds. As Popp himself said, this "waterfall of letters" was supposed to express the fleeting nature of what we think is important. Of course, the irony is that the words disappear before they've even truly appeared. From the very beginning, they are not read as meaningful series of letters, but rather viewed as a fascinating phenomenon. We don't read words made of water. We touch them, we stick our arms into them, we wet our brows with them and we jump through them. Words of water can also be enjoyed from the rear. Like *Text Rain*, *Bit.Fall* invites people to encounter text on a visual actionist level. Meaning plays no role in this encounter. The text doesn't want to be decoded, just seen.

The central, indeed essential characteristic of these cannibalistic text installations is that text is present as non-text and as contradictory presence. The text must remain present behind and specifically in the surprising way it appears, which wows observers. If letters are replaced by sand, as in the 2001 installation *Sand* by Zachary Booth Simpson and Ken Demarest, which otherwise is similar to *Text Rain* in the way it functions and makes observers interact with it, the work loses its anthropophagic basis. Unlike text, sand has no cultural value, and thus as an object of interaction, it cannot appeal to observers as "fallen," symbolically disempowered language.[3]

PORNOGRAPHY AND MUSIC

There is something pornographic—in Frederic Jameson's sense of the visual as per se pornographic[4]—about a text that merely wants to be viewed, not decoded. Like pornography, it encourages enraptured, defenseless gazing. The letters in the text in *Text Rain* and *Bit.Fall* appear in such a way that their physical manifestation can no longer be combined into a statement. They do not want viewers to see beyond them to something they describe. They want to be stared at, hypnotically, as people do when they gaze upon a waterfall or a naked body, from which they can't avert their eyes.

Paradoxically, the hypnotized gaze is also the result of a work that would seem to be the opposite of *Text Rain* or

Bit.Fall. In Bruno Nadeau and Jason Lewis's 2005 installation *Still Standing*, letters lying around on the bottom of the screen form themselves into a short, forty-word text in the silhouette of observers, if they remain standing, motionless, in front of the screen for a few seconds. The text criticizes the befuddlement of our time, which it also seeks to correct by forcing those who would read it to stand still and watch. So is the text, in a kind of reverse cannibalism, exploiting this effect in the interest of the venerable cultural technique of reading?

That is only the case at first glance—the rebellion entailed by the installations described above scarcely extends further than its immediate effect on viewers. Would observers pause to watch for longer, if the text were to be constantly renewed and present 400 or 4,000 words to be read? Technically it would be no problem to follow the eyes of observers and change the silhouetted text before they turn away. But would the text truly have a chance if it were only text? How long can the text extend the immobilization of observers if, as a body that slows itself to be stared at, it disappears behind the world that it opens up? The artists in question don't press the issue. They keep the moment of standing still and reading—or rather looking—for as short a time as possible and in so doing present a text that in its very rebellion kowtows before the anthropophagic effect.

A better metaphor than Jameson's pornography of the visual is the musicalization of the significant. Music, after all, is never about significance and understanding. Musical *music*

sound does not refer to anything beyond itself. It only wants to be perceived in its own physicality. Listening is always staring, which is why in his *Critique of Judgment* Immanuel Kant classified music as one of the "free beauties" that represent nothing.[5]

This metaphor has been popular since Guillaume Apollinaire noted in his 1913 essay "Les peintres cubists" that cubist and "pure" painting was to previous painting as music was to literature. In this sense, in 1930, Méla Balázs described absolute (i.e., abstract) film as "optical music" that doesn't signify anything, but is instead itself "unmediated materialized significance." Writing from the same perspective, Rosalind E. Krauss later understood the abstract painting of the late nineteenth and early twentieth centuries as a striving for the "condition of music," and Martin Seel called actions films "music for the eye."[6] Like color and form in abstract painting, the postalphabetic, anthropophagized text becomes an object to be observed beyond its traditional role as a semantic sign. Its significance is its withdrawal of significance.

VISUALIZATIONS

The musicalization of the text in digital media reverses the original function of those media. In the 1980s, some people understood the computer as the revenge of the word on television. There were no images, to say nothing of moving ones, on computers, and even computer games played themselves out in landscapes of words. In online role playing (the MUDs, MOOs, and MMORPGs), to act was to type.

We didn't stand in front of a house. We read: "You are standing in front of a house." We didn't pick up an ax, or have our avatars do it. We typed in: "Pick up the ax!"

The drive toward images—and an initial cannibalistic impulse within the computer's possibilities for expression—soon expressed itself in the ASCII graphics that were painstaking put together using the keyboard. Less idiosyncratic, but more important for the computer's eventual triumph, was the graphic interface. Since 1984 with the Apple Macintosh, and somewhat later in Microsoft windows, we no longer have to type in "\>copy c:\filename1.doc+filename2.doc a:\trip" to copy two files. We simply click the mouse on the files' icons and drag them into the folder we want. With Adobe, the graphic user interface was followed by desktop publishing, which rescued computers from the confines of spreadsheets à la Lotus and made them appealing to designers. The rest of the story is well known. In the 1990s, still images became an integral part of computers. Then came audio, then video. The visualization of communication in the form of photos and increasingly, as Facebook shows, in videos puts an end to the revenge of the word on television, reversing the situation completely. The *non plus ultra* of this sort of anthropophagic attack is Facebook's feature "Text Delight," which aesthetically embellishes written texts with "funny" bits of animation, for example by adding colorful stars that float up from a pair of opening hands on the bottom margin if users type the words "best wishes."

In digital media, too, the "Gutenberg galaxy" and the "literate monopoly," as theorists Marshall McLuhan and

Friedrich Kittler called the span of time in which the book was the undisputed leading medium of society, are giving way to the culture of the visual. The history of media is shifting from a model of sense to a model of the senses. With images and sounds, the objects are always simply there, whereas text first needs to be decoded. From the perspective of the history of human civilization, this represents a return to an earlier condition of perception at a higher level of technology.

PROGRESS AS RETURN

No matter what in fact existed in the very beginning of everything, at the beginning of the word was the image. Before letters, used together, created series of sounds to stand for an object (*c-o-w* for cow or *d-o-g* for dog), they depicted an object. The letter *A*, which the Phoenicians wrote upside down, imitated an ox: the point was the chin, the horizontal bar the eyes and two tips the horns. Likewise an *M* was a snake. The letter visually presented the object depicted much as children acoustically depict a dog when they call it a "bow-wow." Semioticians would call this visual onomatopoeia and speak of an iconic equivalence of signifier and signified.

Importantly, the sound of an object had no immediate relationship to its representation in writing. Writing did not, as it does today, make language visible. It depicted an object that language represented in its own way: an upside-down *A*, which in Phoenician designated an ox. Only once pictography was replaced by letters and words did the visual and acoustic signifiers converge. The ox head was turned upside down and no longer stood for an ox, but for the sound with which its aural signifier began: the *A* in "aleph." The technical term for this is *acrophony*: the reduction of a sound to its first letter.

This clever bit of shorthand was the beginning of various possibilities for combination. As soon as the visual *A* was no longer an ox head but rather the sound *A*, it could be used to form all possible series of sounds for all possible objects, if it were combined with other visual signs that had been freed from the object they originally designated to become acoustic sounds. Written language no longer needed thousands of characters, as today's Chinese still does, but rather only twenty-five letters, give or take a few, which users could put together as they chose.

Insofar as it increasingly visualizes communication, the computer restores the pictorial nature of the beginning of language. For quite some time, we have no longer needed to describe our avatars on the Internet. We simply display them. In general, we describe what we're doing less and less. Instead, we post photos and videos. The visual is displacing written language. At the same time, the visual and the acoustic are becoming language.

The abstract process of acrophony of yore was taken to another level by the radical reduction of the alphabet and numerals system of signs to binary code. Just as pictograms and syllables evolve into lettered language, this reduction too has radically expanded the capacity of the remaining signs to describe things. Every image and every sound can be expressed as a series of zeros and ones and be communicated, for example, via the telephone.

No matter what happens on its surface, the computer remains essentially and, for most people invisibly, a textual medium. While the old culture of text, as it was known in the Gutenberg galaxy, may be disappearing, we are increasingly becoming surrounded by unseen text. The anthropophagic treatment of text, not just in art installations but in new media generally, recasts it, in an act of parody, as an invisible presence in the "belly" of the computer.

FORM OF SURVIVAL

One artistic commentary on this constellation of text and non-text is a large picture (112 × 406 cm) made of various colored dots from 2007, bearing the title *The Complete Works of W.S.* What looks like a computerized work of abstract pointillism, a visual painting that seeks only to present itself, in reality represents the world of Shakespeare's writings. The artist, Caleb Larsen, actually transformed Shakespeare's collected works into differently colored pixels. Here, the text is consumed in anthropophagic style rather than eradicated. Each color is acrophonically connected to the first letter of its name: *b* for blue, *r* for red, and *g* for green.

Bringing Shakespeare's works—letter by letter, line by line, play by play—yields a collection of colored points that only seems to be random. Observers may simply stare, impressed, at the massive collection of colored dots, but it's anything but what it appears to be: a radical break from the model of sense in favor of the model of the senses. The "point" of this anthropophagic treatment of text is that the text survives within the effect the work produces, as Jonah once survived in the belly of the whale. The text doesn't get lost when it is confined in this way. It can be translated back into its original form at any time with the proper software. Moreover, with a bit of practice, people can actually *read* the picture, pixel for pixel, letter for letter.

The Complete Works of W.S. would be a clever and a paradoxical answer to the question: what book would you take with you to a desert island? This one picture literally speaks louder than a thousand words. All you would have to do is learn to read the language of the colors without the aid of a computer, which presumably would not exist on the island. This picture is perhaps the only image that we could say is entirely free of pornography. Staring at it for hours on a hot island day would entail nothing less than seeing through it in a double sense: through the pixels to the letters, and through the letters to a world that exists only inside Shakespeare and his readers. It would be an attempt to reclaim the Other, which has been devoured by the effect produced by digital media, as one's own.

Marcelo arrived in a black Ford. We followed his route on our mobile phone and went to the elevator when he turned from Planetário de Gávea onto our street. He stopped to wait at the corner on the other side of the street next to all the boxes and bags of garbage that had accumulated over the weekend. A black sedan with tinted windows drove up amid all the noise and the unbearable heat. He signaled to us with his blinkers. It was a bit like a movie, where you never know who is sitting in the car and whether a gun might be involved. We approached the vehicle and, gathering our nerve, opened the doors with an "Oi, Marcelo." The man returned our greeting without turning around: "Oi, Luciana." From the speakers came my favorite song, which Luciana was streaming to the car via Spotify. She saw my surprise and laughed, proud of herself. We settled back into the leather-clad rear seats, while Marcelo handed us two bottles of water. It was really like a movie thriller—despite the water.

COMMUNICATION CAPITALISM

This scene took place in Rio de Janeiro in January 2015, but similar ones play themselves out in Hong Kong, New York, or Madrid several times a day. This is the world of what is euphemistically called the sharing or on-demand economy—the world, to be more precise, of platform and

Sharing econ

communication capitalism. Uber, just like Airbnb, claims to be nothing more than a platform that helps people communicate, in this case people who need a ride and people who have room in their cars. Using this argument, buttressed by buzzwords like *innovation*, *interaction*, and *immersion*, Uber has fended off the mistrust of local commercial regulators and consistently increased its company value. The only major bumps in the road have been the moral failings of some of its managers.

No matter how much talk there is of sharing, or how casually people address one another, this world is still ruled by the iron laws of the market. Of course, the app-based platform is not, as it purports, just an ultramodern tool for the venerable phenomenon of thumbing a ride or picking up a hitchhiker. Traditionally, the drivers were the ones who determined the route and all they asked their passengers to pay was a share of the gas money. For this reason it's hardly surprising that Uber's business model has drawn protest— even from within. In September 2015, Uber drivers in the United States filed a class action suit to force the company to acknowledge that they were employees and not just communication partners. Their argument was that Uber communication actually consists of commands since the company tells its drivers not only which routes to take but how much they can charge. The drivers are not the normal sort of independent service providers, and most likely don't feel as though they're a voluntary part of a grassroots transportation project. For that reason, in America, they wanted to be acknowledged as employees so that they would have access to unemployment and other social benefits. The suit was settled in April 2016 after the company, which is currently valued at between 50 to 70 billion dollars, agreed to pay out the hardly princely sum of 100 million. With that Uber had warded off the greatest danger to its business model: skepticism toward its self-definition as a technological mediation platform. The result of Uber's largesse for the drivers was that they were now allowed to ask customers for a tip, which the company previously had frowned upon, and had the right to ask for justification if their relationship, be it one of labor or merely communication, was in danger of being terminated.

Even less of a surprise is that conventional taxi drivers and their representatives are none too happy about Uber. In September 2016, Britain's National Union of General and Municipal workers succeeded in court where their American counterparts failed. Uber was ordered to offer its drivers a minimum wage, compensation in case of illness, and paid holidays. Taxi drivers have every reason to be enraged. The Californian company undercuts local wage agreements and destroys jobs that at least in well-developed countries offer a measure of security. But that's just the way communication works in today's age of globalization. Regional rules lose their validity, and places are divorced from their history and incorporated into the modus operandi of global companies.

The technical term for this is *corporate nullification*. As a sixteen-wheeler runs over a plastic bottle on the road, Uber simply runs over the specific character of places, including the wage agreements that emerged from past labor battles. On June 2, 2016, the EU's Commission for Internal Market, Industry, Entrepreneurship and SMEs gave a green light to this barreling force, ruling that innovative business models could not be banned to protect existing ones. Member states, the commission decided, "assess the adequacy of their national employment rules considering the different needs of workers and self-employed people in the digital world as well as the innovative nature of collaborative business models." The basic idea was that disruption is part of the developmental laws of the free-market economy and well suited globally to the demands of globalization.[1]

But that commission ran into problems from none other than that EU Legal Commission, which reacted to a complaint by a union of Spanish taxi drivers. In late 2017, the European Court of Justice redefined the communications platform Uber as a transportation service provider subject to all the EU legal and regulatory rules governing that sort of business. In Europe, as was not the case in the United States and the rest of the world, Uber saw the writing on the wall and modified its business model to work together with drivers who possessed a taxi license. For that reason the Court's verdict didn't change much for the company. There was little to fear that left-wing EU governments would demand that the company pay vacation, sickness, and social security compensation to the "independent contractors" with whom it had signed limited employment agreements.

Will it float?

Of course, the issue of drivers' qualifications and wages will become moot once self-driving cars become the norm. Until then, Uber has no choice but to concentrate on surviving as a brand and attracting publicity. In Germany, where there is, of course, no way around taxi licenses, Uber has managed to grow without any drivers of its own. The German Uber is primarily an app for booking standard taxis, and ironically many German taxis driving around cities sport advertisements for the service.

Uber's drive to success emerged from the competition between the political outrage of taxi unions and regional transportation authorities and newly created legal customs, supported by Uber's invocation of petition campaigns from people in various locations who wanted the service to be permitted. That was how Uber proceeded in September 2017 when its London license wasn't renewed. City authorities, the company argued, were giving in to pressure from a small number of critics who wanted to restrict consumer choice. The numbers—Uber claimed to have more than 40,000 drivers and 3.5 million users—and the preponderance of the anecdotal evidence support Uber's claim to have the majority on its side. There are simply too few taxis around, and among the ones that do exist, there are too many unfriendly drivers who listen to music too loud and smoke illicitly in their cars, hoping to cover the smell with clouds of vanilla spray. Against this backdrop, it was easy to depict the authorities as choking off innovation and Uber's conquest of the market as a victory for the culture of participation or for civil disobedience—in Uber's home country, the company is even sometimes stylized as an antigovernment movement. The fact that in many places taxis are controlled by virtual mafias and drivers earn less than minimum wage only bolstered neoliberal arguments that Uber was sticking up for labor freedom and unfettered competition.

This situation changes immediately and tragically when Uber cars outnumber regular taxis in a city. "Companies do not care how they abuse us just so the executives get their bonuses," wrote New York City taxi driver Doug Schifter on Facebook before taking his own life on February 5, 2018. "They count their money, and we are driven down into the streets we drive, becoming homeless and hungry. I will not be a slave working for chump change. I would rather be dead."[2]

The symbolic location Schifter chose for his suicide was in front of City Hall. This is where Uber lobbyists gain the concessions that give the company an advantage over conventional taxi firms. Lobbying is Uber's primary area of investment, and the company specializes in recruiting former government regulators who know their way around state and municipal rules. The fact that a number of former Uber lobbyists worked for the Obama administration reminds us that the Republicans aren't the only political party that puts workers' rights on the back burner. Indeed, what was once the Democrats' great moral capital vis-à-vis their rivals, Roosevelt's New Deal, is in jeopardy. As the New York Times wrote in 2017: "Uber and the like may be taking the economy back toward a pre–New Deal era when businesses had enormous power over workers and few checks on their ability to exploit it."[3]

It's hardly shocking, then, that resistance to Uber has taken on threatening dimensions in some places. One piece of anecdotal evidences was an Uber driver in Buenos Aires who asked me to sit up front with him, thus splitting up the couple who had just been enjoying an intimate warm summer's night dancing the tango on the Plaza Dorrego. He wanted it to look as though he were a designated driver chauffeuring friends home after a joint evening out. In Argentina, we learned, taxi drivers joined with the police to lie in wait for Uber cars. He didn't tell us precisely what he meant by that, but it was clear that if we were stopped, the police wouldn't have a hard time telling we weren't old school chums since we spoke as little Spanish as our driver did English. After being immersed in the playful melancholy of the tango only minutes ago, we suddenly felt the frisson of the illicit much as we had two years earlier with Marcelo. Only this time, we weren't concealed behind tinted windows. We were supposed to sit in plain sight chatting away with our "friend," the driver.

DISRUPTIVE MEDIA

Of course, it makes little sense to blame Uber drivers for such processes of monopolization. After all, they may only being trying to survive, having lost their decently paying hotel job, with vacation and health benefits, to Airbnb or having been fired because clickworkers are cheaper. The absurd thing about the sharing economy, and the secret to its success, is its ability to pass off the dismantlement of social welfare measures as social opportunity. In this narrative, citizens are helping one another to break the monopolies of the taxi and hotel companies.

Moreover, the service providers, it is argued, enjoy unprecedented independence and flexibility. There is a lot of talk about the freedom such flexible working conditions offer workers. That may remind some of us of Marx's dictum of "doubly free labor," which frees workers from feudal and caste restrictions while also leaving them free from any ownership in the means of production—and thus entirely subject to the conditions of the market. Over the course of history, trade unions arose to better these workers' lots, negotiating labor agreements that "restricted" their double freedom, for instance, by setting a minimum wage below which they were not allowed to offer their services. The sharing economy and platform capitalism, on the other hand, free people from these beneficial restrictions, allowing them to offer their services at cut-rate prices depending on the market with no regard to wage agreements. The rise of the "gig economy" makes it necessary to update Karl Marx's idea to one of "triply free labor"—free of constraints, free of ownership, and free of any genuine employment contracts. Personifying this triple freedom are Uber's partners on the street, the so-called independent contractors: people who, in Uber's eyes, merely drive through our cities when and where they want to and sometimes enter into micro-contracts with strangers they meet on their way. Who could possibly have anything against that?

The situation is reminiscent of Germany after the fall of the Berlin Wall, when East Germans only bought products from the West, thus reducing their own industries' chances of survival. The difference is that back then some of the money that was lost eventually returned in the form of government spending to cover the unemployment pay for those who lost their jobs and to help rebuild eastern Germany economically. By contrast the 20 percent that Uber charges drivers for communication facilitation either stays entirely in California or is reinvested in the global expansion of the brand. This is an example of "disruptive innovation," a term coined in 1995 by economist Clayton Christensen to refer to the displacement of established technology and products in the lower price segment by alternatives and the transformation of nonconsumers into consumers. This description may not apply entirely to Uber, which started out focusing on luxury cars and first of all concentrated on turning non–service providers into service providers. Nonetheless, there is no doubt that Uber is extremely innovative and extremely disruptive.[4]

Generally speaking, disruption is a central characteristic of platforms like Uber that connect communication partners in a way that separates them from existing forms of communication—just like Google, which connects us innovatively and comfortably with the knowledge of the world while divorcing us from libraries and encyclopedias, or like social networks, which bind us in new ways with friends, acquaintances, or even perfect strangers and disrupt traditional forms of communication like conversing with a friends in a bar or a seat neighbor on a train. What all of these separating newfangled connections have in common is the replacement of a local, direct, holistic relationship with a mediated, segmented, remote-controlled one. The consequences are both psychological and economic. Nowadays, people may only tell their friends about their vacation on Facebook, or only be able to connect with their customers around the corner by way of California—and under California's terms.

Uber has become a paradigm of this sort of disruptive innovation—and a signifier for a dark future as studies like Gary Hall's *The Uberfication of the University* (2016) or Trebor Scholz's *Uberworked and Underpaid: How Workers Are Disrupting the Digital Economy* (2017) demonstrate. Hall argues that the model of "microentrepreneurs of the self" associated with Uber and the sharing economy even threatens universities, because academics, forced to work under restricted contracts and subject to rigid ranking procedures, live in permanent fear of falling and staying below the poverty line. Scholz associates Uber with "wage theft" and "crowd fleecing" and pleads for a "preemptive strike against an Uber-ized future" through "platform co-ops" that collectivize the model of platform capitalists.[5]

Such collectivization would—notably—not have to resort to the confiscation of private property. When the means of production are nothing more than a software developed into a communication platform, critics can just copy it. The question, as is always the case with ideas of resistance and rescue, is how many of the 40,000 Uber drivers and 3.5 million users in London (or the untold millions throughout the world) will take part. If they don't migrate to a fairer and more sustainable "ride service," the socially just alternative won't stand a chance. The transition should work better than has been the case with Facebook, which has easily withstood attacks by Google+, Ello, or Diaspora. Or WhatsApp, which people still use despite the data protection concerns because everyone they know is on it. However, until ride seekers and providers prove the contrary, Uber will be the only real game in town.

CONTROLLED DRIVING

Of course, almost no one stops to consider wage agreements, (self-)exploitation, and social harmony, when they call an Uber. Nor does anyone think about what Uber embodies. After all, the threat it poses to regular jobs governed by wage agreements is only one of Uber's several destructive innovations. For instance, the adjustment of prices according to momentary demand entails a change from regulated tariffs based on the amount of labor and expenses involved to purely market-oriented prices. This change may be easy to justify—who minds paying a couple of dollars more for a service, if he or she doesn't have to stand out in the rain. Yet this could turn out to be the preliminary stage of a procedure by which customers make offers and the ones willing and able to pay the most enjoy an advantage. Customers' wealth would determine whether they got access to the service desired and undermine the sense of social solidarity of people waiting their turn at a taxi stand. That's not really a problem, many people might say. Individuals have to know how much a given service is worth to them. Anyone who doesn't have enough money can always take the bus—providing there still is one.

But social conflict caused by flexible prices is just one of the problems that the future, which Uber is already forcing, holds in store. A far more serious one is the undermining of data protection and privacy that happens with every Uber trip. The movements of individuals in a city are made available for data analysis. Uber, and who knows who else, knows how often and how long its clients visit other people. The result, if we take the most harmless situation, could be a personal, memory-aiding log book, a personal urban travelogue as an Excel spreadsheet that clients might be given as a gift after five years of being loyal customers. The probably less-welcomed map will include all the places one has been for one-night stands that felt wrong even before sunrise.[6]

Symptomatic of the development of a society that controls individuals is the acceptance of decreasing privacy in return for increasing comfort. People don't want to get in a taxi they hail on street any more, just as they don't want to go to any old restaurant by the side of the road but only one that's recommended by Yelp, Wallpaper*, or TripAdvisor. It's reassuring to know in which direction the taxi is coming and precisely when it will arrive, as well as the name and average rating of the driver and what music can be expected if you use the Spotify service. It's reassuring not to worry in foreign countries whether you can make yourself understood or whether the driver is taking a longer route to your destination to drive up the fare. The app clears up all these questions and documents them in black and white, thereby taming the unknown that used to always be part of traveling. In the process, the world, be it Shanghai, Nairobi, Rio, or Istanbul, is kept in line by the extended eye of Silicon Valley. People collaborate with the society of monitoring and control because they themselves like having things under *their* control. Nothing symbolizes this new power better than the God's-eye point of view the app offers on the car you've ordered as it approaches. Before it even arrives, you're able to form your own opinion about the intelligence of the driver.

The unavoidable reverse side of the coin with this business model is that the driver has not only my destination on his display screen, but my name and average rating. If the taxi company Uber wants to pass itself off as a communications platform, there needs to be communicative equality—not only the driver has to prove he's worthy, but customers as well. The inevitable by-product is that customers are on their best behavior lest they be unable to find a driver the next time. Trapped in the clutches of the economy of reputation, we finally stop burping in taxis and make doubly sure to leave the toilet clean at the homes of our Airbnb or Couchsurfing hosts. The society of control is always a society of disciplinary measures, as well.

THE OBSERVED OBSERVER

The disciplining of the customer begins with the power he is granted over the driver. Just try to book a return trip if you haven't given the driver of the first leg a rating. Customers have a duty to rank and rate, as Uber has installed an algorithm that denies service if clients fall behind in their evaluations. That may not be a problem for people who have learned over the course of their "social web" life to give feedback whenever told to. When there are no more gatekeepers, everyone has to stand in for them.

Nonetheless, it is striking that customers are asked to justify themselves for handing out less-than-perfect ratings. If you only give four ("Good") and not five ("Excellent") stars, you have to explain yourself ("What went wrong?") or at least tick one of the predetermined explanatory categories (punctuality, driving style, service, price, vehicle condition, other). This may seem like a pitiless meritocracy, and it's rumored that drivers with an average rating of less than 4.5 run the risk of being excommunicated. On the other hand, perhaps all that's behind this is the common curiosity that seems to have prepossessed everyone in the big data age. We all want to know as much as humanly possible about everyone else. Thus, it hardly amazes that since late 2016 Uber even demands justifications for excellent ratings: "What went well?"

Within such a system of control, it's easier to complain than to refuse to communicate. For example, about the price: it's well known that you don't talk about money in an Uber car, so sometimes you only learn whether the costs are the same as the estimate once you get out of the vehicle. The only way to register a dispute is via the app's evaluation menu, and experience shows that this happens very efficiently. As you would expect from a communication business, you get an immediate reaction, the price difference is credited in around five minutes, and a quarter of an hour later you receive an email explaining the problem. Perhaps the driver didn't know his way and failed to take the shortest route. You're also told that the driver will be informed about your complaint "for improvement and to provide a better experience in the future." That can be a bit unsettling; you may feel sympathy with the driver. It also raises other questions. Will he pick me up next time? Will he tell other drivers about me? Will Uber class me as a malcontent in future?

Naturally it's part of the communications platform's standard operating procedure to send you an email two days later asking you to rate Uber's handling of the "recent Uber issue." This is perhaps the most delicate of the entire procedure of contacting the platform. Is it okay to just ignore/click away such messages as you would other unsolicited mails? Or is there an internal record of how willing to communicate you are? Maybe there's even a blacklist for recalcitrants who will be forced to wait twice as long the next time they call for an Uber or be completely ignored for a while as punishment. Once it became known that Uber uses "Greyball" software to block certain users (in particular official monitors) from the app, such measures of retribution began to seem like a realistic threat.[7]

Hassling people to give ratings is a defining characteristic of other platform companies as well, of course. With Airbnb, hardly have you checked out of an apartment when you get an email asking for your feedback: "You just checked out of Monique's place. Now, take a minute to reflect on the experience and share a quick review. You'll have space to leave private feedback, just for Monique, and public comments for future guests too. We won't share any of your responses until after Monique leaves feedback too." You might ignore that mail—maybe because you're busy planning your next trip—when a message arrives that Monique has rated you.

Naturally, you can only read it once you've done your duty and ranked her—or the rating period has expired. Until that happens, Airbnb repeatedly sends you "invitations" to evaluate. If you studiously ignore them, the platform will finally declare: "Now that the review period is over, we've posted Monique's review to your Airbnb profile. While it's too late to write a review of your own, you can send your feedback to Monique using your Airbnb message thread." Communication is everything. And the clearer that is, the worse your conscience at your own unwillingness to cooperate—and your fear again that you could end up on a blacklist.

SOCIAL SCORE BLUEPRINT

Without doubt, communications platforms like Uber and Airbnb are aggressive about getting you to communicate, and there's an insidious reason why. No matter how negatively I might rate a given driver or landlord, I give positive feedback to the rating procedure as such, which accrues authority should I ever be the object of a complaint. Every criticism of a driver and every word of praise for a landlord potentially justifies the platform disciplining you yourself someday. If there are to be ratings, then let everyone make them. That's the way twenty-first-century democracy works.

It's only logical, then, that many observers hold up Uber as a pioneer of an effective economy of reputation, in which providers of poor service are taken out of circulation. "Drivers who provide poor service are eliminated," gushed the Internet innovator and inventor of the phrase "Web 2.0" Tim O'Reilly in 2013. "As users of these services can attest, reputation does a better job of ensuring a superb customer experience than any amount of government regulation. Governments should be studying these models, not fighting them, and adopting them where there are no demonstrable ill effects."[8]

Three years after O'Reilly's statement, the satirical British science-fiction series *Black Mirror* played through the unsavory effects that the principle of regulation by reputation could have. The first episode from the third season, entitled "Nosedive," presents a world in which everyone rates everyone for everything all the time: in taxis, at the ticket counter, in the elevator, and at parties. Wherever people interact with one another, they can give others one to five stars. Those with an average rating of below 4.2, or even 4.5, can be denied access to certain public spaces, services, or privileges, for instance a seat on an alternative to a canceled flight or a discount on their rent. The result is that people begin being more friendly—although in an obviously transparent fashion—to everyone else. Everyone is degraded to the level of a number—an average rating hovering visibly beside their heads—whose generation and justification is deeply dubious. As a result, people only perceive others as those numbers and decide on that basis whether they want to interact with them.

Critics reviewing this episode rightly pointed out the similarity to the American rating app Peeple, a.k.a. "Yelp for people." And a former Facebook manager who helped popularize the like button also found that the episode reminded her of the wave of social-media metrics unleashed by that innovation. "That haunts me on a pretty regular basis," she was quoted as saying. "Because it's not that far off."[9]

The rule of nature, history, and philosophy, "ex orient lux," also applies to technological matters. The future of the West is being born in the Far East. In China, a social credit system is already a part of the thirteenth Five-Year Plan, according to which by 2020 the entire country is supposed to be connected to a network of wide-ranging ratings that will decide people's careers, access to school, services, travel visas, and even modes of transport. In China, people think twice not only about criticizing the system on Weibo or other social networks, but also about crossing the street against a red light. Even if no car is approaching, an employee of the Ministry for Social Credit could be standing on the corner or a camera could identify me even before I have crossed the road. People are also encouraged to regularly visit their parents and not to spend ten hours a day playing computer games. In their ratings, socially irresponsible behavior can be a strike against you, as can certain political attitudes.

Along with criticism of opponents of the regime, reports about China's social-credit system often depict satisfied "normal citizens" happy to appear on the list of the best people in the village, who are glad to hang the stars they are given over the gates to their courtyards and who are convinced that people are now more friendly and behave more considerately toward one another. They would not call their society a conformist nightmare, but rather, had they read Ernst Bloch, a utopia of social order. Indeed, this procedure seems well suited to administer to approximately 1.4 billion people and could also be used in countries with smaller populations and greater democracy. In the end, it's nothing more than the logical extension and intensification of the culture of transparency that inspires social networks in the West and companies like Airbnb and Uber.

China gives the West a view of its own future, in which one day people will only smile when they remember the hesitant first steps of insurance companies and other service providers in offering price rebates for defensive driving and healthy lifestyles. How small-minded is it, in light of China's gigantic project, to criticize groundbreaking companies like Uber for hushing up the fact that in October 2016 the names, email addresses, and telephone numbers of 57 million customers world-wide were stolen?[10] Or that the firm reached an irresponsible deal with the hackers to the detriment of those same customers?

GLOCALIZATION

Hong Kong, 2016. Anyone who lives in this city appreciates Uber. Taxis are like the ambassadors of a city, the things that welcome you at an airport or train station and make a first impression. In Germany, that impression is the comfort of a Mercedes. In Hong Kong, where every second car is either a Mercedes or a BMW, the taxis are all, without exception, old Toyotas. It must cost a fortune to keep such a fleet of vintage cars on the road. Taxi drivers rent these cars, and that explains why the vehicles aren't maintained or equipped with scanners to pay tolls. Taxi drivers pay the tolls the old-fashioned way, by tossing change out the window and then charging customers individually. Another problem is that of the service restrictions between Hong Kong Island and the Kowloon peninsula, which often require you to change taxis at a predetermined transfer location in order to get where you need to go. Such deficiencies make Uber, which simply conveys you from point A to point B without any discussion, very attractive.

Insofar as it eradicates local working people's shortcomings but not their achievements, there is a positive side to the ways in which global platform capitalism gets rid of regional peculiarities. With Uber you can take a taxi in Hong Kong that's clean and quiet and doesn't have a driver constantly belching and counting up the fares he's taken in that day. With Uber you can take a taxi in Prague without being overcharged, and you can take one in Rio without being driven by someone who's watching telenovelas on his or her dashboard monitor. With Uber, you're safer here, more comfortable there, and occasionally you can even save a bit of money.

Ande de Taxi legal!—take a legal cab! These words can be seen in the back windows of many taxis in Rio. They carry a dual meaning since "legal" is, rather counterintuitively, local slang for "cool." The campaign aims to convince people that vehicles operated by licensed taxi drivers are truly cool—and not Marcelo's car with its tinted windows and possible pistol in the glove compartment. We now take a lot of legal taxis in Rio, although the main reason is that Luciana repeatedly had to cancel Ubers because the drivers weren't able to read their maps and drove blindly past the pre-agreed meeting point. A two-minute wait can easily turn into a ten-minute one. And it's anything but cool to stand by the side of the road for what feels like an eternity waiting for an Uber while empty taxis constantly cruise past.

And that's not all. You'd have to wait a long time to get one of the first-generation Uber drivers like Marcelo with his firearm, black gloves, and bottles of water. A new generation of Uber drivers has arrived. Kids who couldn't find the city center without GPS. Kids who text while driving, whose cars smell like vanilla although they don't even smoke, and who force their customers to put up with insipid Brazilian or Asian or European pop ditties. A new caste of people with all the old flaws. The Marcelos have disappeared. There's no vague whiff of Mafia cool—just the feeling that you're being taken for a ride.

But why should a disruptive innovation end up any differently than a subculture? As soon as it goes mainstream, it loses its edgy appeal. Drivers and customers no longer feel like guests at an underground, unlicensed party, but like drivers and customers. You don't bother talking about this once-so-illicit-seeming service that fit so well with your lifestyle. Conversation is restricted to the same three formulaic sentences when the customers get in the car. Lucianna? Marcelo? How's it going? Good, and you? You might exchange a few words about the route or whether the music is too loud or the AC turned up too high. But that's it. The silence persists until the end of the trip when the customers get out. Take care, Marcelo. Yeah, you too. The only excitement Uber offers these days is watching the Uber map and wagering with friends about whether their Uber, which is supposedly only two minutes away, really will arrive before your Uber, which according to the map still needs five.

Only idealists will be astonished by this development. Even if in the beginning Uber was conceived as a modern ride-hitching service and, as was the case with hitchhiking, people tended to talk with one another during trips, everyone knew the ultimate point was making money and not making friends. And since the app took care of directions and obviated any questions of tipping, it was only to be expected that people talk even less in Ubers than in taxis. After all, most regular taxi drivers consider talking and listening to be part of their jobs and good ways of getting a better tip. For that reason, too, Luciana and I are again taking more "cool" cabs. That has no doubt gotten us on another blacklist. Uber surely knows that we hardly use the service anymore and is sure to have noted our infidelity.

RESISTANCE

One evening in Hong Kong, one of the non-Marcelos was driving us home and took the wrong exit off the highway. What's more, the road to our neighborhood was closed off—it was Wednesday, the day of the horse races in Happy Valley. Were we at fault? Was our driver? He should have known this. And we could have told him. Whatever the case may have been, a detour was unavoidable. But then the driver missed the turn-off for Blue Pool Road and had to take another detour straight down the always jam-packed Tai Hang Road. In the end, our trip took half an hour longer and cost twenty Hong Kong dollars more than it should have. It wasn't our fault that the driver couldn't find the right street, we thought once we were home. Every regular taxi driver turns off his meter when he takes a wrong turn. And this, after all, was supposed to be a luxury service.

But then we thought about *Black Mirror* and the 4.5-star bottom limit for Uber drivers. We thought about the heartlessness of radical meritocracy and all the mistakes we had made in our lives. We thought about our mothers and even about the driver's ridiculous fondness for kitschy K-pop—and gave him a top rating. We felt like heroes. We had overcome our baser impulses. We refused to report what had gone wrong and left open what had gone right. We were lying to a system on behalf of its most immediate victims. For a brief moment, we asked ourselves: What would happen if Uber noticed the route, which crassly diverged from the destination we had provided? Would we, together with the driver, be banned without any warning or rationale? But then we looked at one another and knew. It was the right thing to do, even if we had to put up with a couple of wrong turns.

7 THE DEATH ALGORITHM

The survival of digital technologies has always largely depended on their killer instinct. Email communication, for instance, would never have been successful had it not solved the problem of spam. The famous algorithm that remedied the situation was called "SpamAssassin"—a martial name for a filter designed to reduce the white noise in this new medium of communication by separating desirable messages from junk mail. Regardless of what it was called, the elimination of spam was an indispensable prerequisite for digital communication and the popularization of social media.

The first training ground for artificial intelligence is waste disposal. This is where software learns to recognize patterns and classify objects; this is where it makes decisions first about the same situations, then about similar ones, both under supervision and eventually unchecked by humans. All existing and future fantasies concerning intelligent refrigerators, self-driving cars, autonomous robots, and other forms of artificial intelligence that currently excite or frighten the public originate in the "deep learning" model of the junk-mail killer.

The SpamAssassin's kid brother, the "death algorithm," decides, in case a self-driving car encounters an emergency, whether to plow into a group of pedestrians, a mother and child, or a brick wall. This death algorithm has given rise to heated philosophical and legal discussions, all the more so as it is now considered certain that self-driving cars will soon be upon us—sooner, in fact, than autonomous weapons or mechanical pets. This is a politically loaded development, considering the assumption that self-driving cars will not only drastically lower travel costs and energy consumption but also slash the number of accidents. The computer has the driving experiences of all computers at its disposal. It's far quicker at processing far more information than a human driver, and it never gets tired, drives drunk, or texts anyone from behind the wheel. It would be morally irresponsible not to introduce self-driving cars.

Nonetheless, it is also certain that fatal accidents will continue and that self-driven cars will thus have to make decisions that cost some people their lives while sparing others. This brings up the moral dilemma that the death algorithm needs to be equipped with a certain kind of ethics. In this sense, philosophy may become the most important element in in the production chain of an automobile.

TERMINATOR 6

In what is possibly the most famous unauthorized commercial, a car is driving through a landscape obviously from the past. All the people working by the roadside pause to stare in awe at what eventually turns out to be a modern Mercedes luxury sedan, which soon screeches to a halt in front of two little girls playing in the street. The braking action is triggered by a sensor that detects objects in the path of the vehicle. When the car continues on its journey, a boy running with a kite appears, and a young woman looks fondly after him while hanging her laundry. This time, to our surprise, the car hits the child. Did the sensor fail this time?

The answer is given in small, rapid chunks: For a millisecond, just before the impact, we glimpse an image of Hitler, then the startled woman with the laundry basket cries: "Adolf?" The town sign says "Braunau am Inn," and the image fades to a slogan advertising Mercedes' collision prevention system: "Detects dangers before they arise." A final overhead shot reveals the knocked-down boy's twisted limbs splayed out in the shape of a swastika.[1]

This 2013 video clip attracted more than 5 million views by spring 2016—more than 21,000 viewers liked it, some 2,000 disliked it, and the roughly 2,500 comments were split along the same lines. The clip stirred up a certain public controversy, since it promotes the killing of a child who might grow up to become a mass murderer. Of course this is not an authorized Mercedes commercial—it's a graduation project made by students at the Ludwigsburg Film Academy. But neither that nor the indication that the entire episode is fictional has any bearing on the philosophical problem here. In what conditions is it permissible to kill in order to save lives?

The video plays on a trope of pop culture by sending the Mercedes back in time, just as Skynet once dispatched the Terminator, to nip an undesirable historical development in the bud. However, while traveling to the past remains pure science fiction, jumping into the future is gradually becoming part of our reality in the form of predictive analytics. In its variant as "predictive policing," it is already being applied in many places in everyday law-enforcement work. Unlike the procedure in Steven Spielberg's *Minority Report*, the real thing does not rely on the precognitive powers of three mutant humans suspended in a liquid, but on big data mining: establishing crime profiles, correlations, and probability curves that allow the police to "calculate" when and where the next offense will take place.

If this kind of statistical analysis is combined with an individual's genetic makeup, video and reading habits, friend lists, daily routines, and movement profiles as well as posts, likes, shares, comments, and other communicative acts, and then appropriately extrapolated, it may well soon enable a precise prediction of a person's development, including the potential threat she or he poses to society. Equipped with this kind of data, the Mercedes would have science on its side, if it were to drive through Braunau and run over the young Hitler.

OFFSETTING LIFE VALUES

German law includes no provisions permitting the killing of future mass murderers. Sooth-saying does not constitute a legal justification, and predictions resulting from big data mining are not yet considered scientifically valid. In addition, Germans maintain a steadfast faith in education. If time travel to the past were possible, the Mercedes driving through Braunau would likely be occupied by a social worker armed with a package of measures designed to get young

Adolf onto the right track—so he would, for instance, grow up to be an artist rather than a dictator.

Nonetheless, the question of whether it's permissible to kill in order to save lives has long since been debated at the core of our society. Ferdinand von Schirach's courtroom theatrical drama *Terror*, for instance, has the audience sit in judgment on a major in Germany's Bundeswehr who, acting on his own authority, shot down an airliner hijacked by a terrorist. In a quantitative decision, the fictional officer sacrificed the 164 people on the plane in order to save the 70,000 people in Munich's Allianz stadium, where the terrorist intended to crash the passenger jet. In thirty-eight German stage productions during the 2015–16 and 2016–17 seasons, the decision whether the major should be charged with multiple counts of murder for his actions was delegated to the audience, the "real" grand jury in this thought experiment. The televised version of the play, broadcast on October 18, 2016, was the number one event for the public TV channels ARD, ORF, and SRF in Germany, Austria, and Switzerland: the audience got to vote, and the broadcast was followed by a debate on the talk show *Hart aber fair* (Tough but fair). Entrusting the verdict to the public had less to do with the aesthetics of participation than with experimental ethics, which works with empirical studies instead of contenting itself with theoretical conclusions of "armchair philosophy." These days it's not the best argument that usually wins, but rather the majority. At the very least it has become hard to argue without the backing of numbers.[2]

The audience's votes generally resulted in an acquittal—which shows the majority of theatergoers (60 percent) and TV viewers (87 percent) in Germany think or feel unconstitutionally. It is, after all, at odds with the opening article of the German Constitution on the inviolability of human dignity to weigh lives against lives and kill a few innocent people in order to save many more. Contrary to the moral impulses of the majority of the country's citizens, the ethical foundation of German law holds that the lesser of two evils cannot be determined either by mathematical means or by discrimination according to age, gender, or cultural values. The lives of ten people are not worth more than the lives of two, and the life of a child has no more value than that of an old man. The ethics of the nonnegotiable subject prohibit the reduction of a human being to a means to save others, so starving castaways, for instance, are not allowed to kill the weakest, not even a dying member of their group, to increase their own chances of survival. It is only permissible to eat other people if they offer up themselves or agree to submit to a lottery—as in Herman Melville's *Moby-Dick*, Edgar Allan Poe's *Narrative of Arthur Gordon Pym of Nantucket*, and many other seafarers' tales.

With its prohibition on objectifying or instrumentalizing human beings, the German Constitution favors (deontological) duty- or conviction-based ethics over (consequentialist) utilitarian or responsibility-based ethics. While the latter focuses on the result and considers the sacrifice of the few for the salvation of the many justifiable, the former is concerned with the action itself (in the case at hand, the major's decision to shoot down the plane) and puts more stock in the (negative) duty not to kill anyone than in the (positive) duty to save people's lives. This is why, in February 2006, Germany's Federal Constitutional Court quashed section 14, paragraph 3 of the Aviation Security Act passed by the Bundestag one year earlier—a provision that would have permitted the Bundeswehr to shoot down commercial airliners hijacked by terrorists as a last resort—as a violation of the constitutional guarantee of the dignity of human life.

In philosophy, the dilemma of killing in order to save lives is often framed as the "trolley problem." In it, a runaway trolley threatens to kill five people on the tracks, and the only option an observer standing by the switching lever has is to divert the trolley to a side track, where it would only kill *one* person. The decision to kill implied in the pulling of the lever more explicit in the "fat man" variant, in which the trolley may be stopped by pushing—possibly after a fierce struggle—a fat man from a bridge onto the tracks.

THE TROLLEY PROBLEM AFTER 9/11

Schirach's courtroom drama transposes this ethical thought experiment into the post-9/11 era, as does Gavin Hood's film *Eye in the Sky* (2015). This latter story raises the question of whether the life of an innocent girl may be sacrificed to prevent a terrorist attack in Nairobi by means of a drone strike, which would save the lives of at least eighty people, including, most likely, several girls of the same age. The discussion among the responsible parties sitting in front of computer screens in London and Nevada vividly translates the deontological and consequentialist arguments into the accessible medium of film, with moving scenes from the life of the girl and a race against the clock to lure her away from the proposed point of impact. The attempts to save her fail. The girl dies as a result of the drone strike. From the soldiers' point of view—in Hood's film as in Schirach's drama—this collateral damage is an acceptable price to pay for preventing a greater number of casualties. Soldiers, after all, know that in real combat situations civilian casualties are also unavoidable. The difference—indeed the crux of the film—is that, in combat, civilian casualties *happen*, whereas here, with all the data about the situation and its consequences at hand, someone is deliberately *sacrificed*. This is regrettable, but, in terms of an ethics of responsibility, morally justifiable.

Philosophical thought experiments do not bother with compromise. That is what distinguishes them from real life and its fictional representation. Schirach's drama, for instance, includes the argument that by shooting down the plane the major prevented the possibility that the passengers might overpower the terrorist in time or that the Allianz stadium might be evacuated before the crash. Speculating about the possibility of a good outcome or the imponderables of the real damage is a deontological diversionary maneuver to cop out of making a decision. Hood's film, which refuses to supply a happy ending with the salvation of the girl, deserves a lot of credit for fostering interest in the debate at hand.

The logic of the trolley problem only allows for a happy ending in terms of self-sacrifice: if the fat man jumps of his own volition or if you yourself lie down on the tracks. Schirach's major did not have that option. In Hood's film, the Kenyan counterterrorism agent on the ground risks his own life to save the girl's. We may get an opportunity to sacrifice ourselves if, in the event of an accident, we are faced with the option of crashing our car into a single adult rather than many children (or a single child rather than many adults), and instead head straight for the brick wall—only then will we find out whether we possess sufficient courage. That is, at least, what the situation has been so far. Once algorithms take the wheel it will be quite a different matter.

HOMICIDAL VARIANTS

As yet, no movie exists on this subject, but there is a vigorous ongoing debate about the criteria that algorithms in autonomous vehicles will apply to make life-and-death decisions when the options of child, old man, and brick wall present themselves. In May 2016, Germany's federal minister of transport established a committee chaired by a former judge of the Federal Constitutional Court to resolve "ethical questions involved in the paradigm shift from human driver to autopilot." In June 2017, the committee found that in the case of an unavoidable accident, "any differentiation based on personal characteristics (age, sex, physical or mental constitution) is strictly prohibited, as was any "calculation of the numbers of victims," since the individual life was "sacrosanct."[3]

By contrast, in its "Moral Machine"—a platform in which thirteen dilemma scenarios force users to make decisions—MIT is experimenting with all sorts of differentiations. The scenarios include not only the common choice between the death of a single driver versus that of five pedestrians, or of three women and two children versus five senior citizens. Respondents must also decide between four passengers versus four pedestrians crossing the road against the red light, or three criminals and a homeless person versus two doctors and two women. The Moral Machine is presented as a "platform for gathering a human perspective on moral decisions made by machine intelligence, such as self-driving cars" and confronts users with possibly the world's most bizarre moral dilemma, asking them to choose between the lives of two homeless passengers and two female jaywalkers. The US National Highway Safety Administration apparently also sees the need for considering such moral dilemmas. In its 116-page "Federal Automated Vehicles Policy" of September 2016, under the heading "Ethical Considerations," the agency wrote: "Algorithms for resolving these conflict situations should be developed transparently using input from Federal and State regulators, drivers, passengers and vulnerable road users, and taking into account the consequences of an HAV's actions on others."[4]

The manufacturers themselves are still staying out of the real debate, preferring instead to focus entirely on technological challenges or legal parameters. Occasionally they even cast doubt on the necessity of a debate and dismiss the question by arguing that if self-driving cars have time enough to make these kinds of decisions, they will also have time enough to brake, especially since they are rigorously programmed for low-risk driving. Those of us, however, who put more faith in gravity than in gravitas will be skeptical about such solutions and may even find that the combination of interconnectedness and speed *within* the car creates a dilemma that is far more complex than the trolley problem. Rather like the Moral Machine, that dilemma replaces clinical abstraction with contextual knowledge.

Let's picture the following scenario in the not-too-distant future: A boy flying his drone runs into the street, straight in front of an autonomously driving Mercedes. Within split seconds the on-board computer will know, thanks to facial recognition and data mining on the Internet, that doctors have given the woman by the roadside a life expectancy of ten months, that the cyclist next to her has two small children, that a third bystander is the sole child of a care-dependent woman, and that the only direction to swerve in that is not occupied by a person would send the car through a rickety bridge railing and down 160 feet onto the railway lines.

No matter what decision the computer makes and what part the insights gleaned from the Internet play in it, unconstitutionality comes into it long before the comparative analysis of life values takes place in the moment of danger. Once they have assessed the situation, the algorithms will make their decision based on the if-then logic they were programmed with. Some cars, then, might not bother to

> deliberate, unre reflex

avoid the child causing the accident (especially if it is a teen-ager playing Pokémon Go on his phone, and if there are other children in the car); others might go straight for the soon-to-die woman; yet others might head for the railing. The violation of the law resides in this preliminary decision, since it is taken—unlike the reflex-like reaction of a human driver (which scarcely qualifies as a decision)—deliberately and in cold blood. The life-and-death decision in this hypo-thetical emergency was made long before that fateful drive, maybe on a lovely summer's day in the park when the own-ers were selecting the various features of their new car on their smartphone and, having picked the color and the type of upholstery, also chose, with a tap of the finger, the death algorithm of their preference.

The new technologies bring along ethical, psychologi-cal, and political conundrums that would have been utterly incomprehensible only yesterday: Who will program the death algorithms in our cars? Will the vehicles' owners have a choice? Will the choice remain with the car-manufacturer? Will there be different algorithms for different categories of vehicles? For different brands of cars? For different coun-tries? Will politics take this decision away from business and (following a referendum) impose a specific algorithm? Will each country have its own algorithm? Will there be a UN resolution—and a black market?

The obvious view is that the ethical equipment of a car must not be left up to the manufacturer but ought to be sub-ject to society's laws. Otherwise, corporations might seek to gain a competitive advantage by making morally dubious promises, for instance by promoting their cars, as Mercedes did in October 2016, with the claim that, in an emergency, they would prioritize the occupants' safety. Tough luck for the inattentive kid in the street, whether his name is Adolf or not. Empirical studies show that most interviewees do favor sacrificing the lives of the car's occupants in an emergency and saving the lives of others. However, if the question is phrased in a slightly different way, their view changes: SUV drivers are not alone in saying that they wouldn't buy a car programmed with exactly this kind of victim-oriented ethics.[5]

As soon as this elephant in the room is discussed, there seems to be no conceivable solution other than egoism. Why would you want to invest "good money" in a vehicle that promises to put other people's interests above your own in an emergency? And yet: Could there be a way to reconcile these two views? Is the acquittal of Schirach's major in German theaters the first step to a referendum that will culminate in the consent to self-sacrifice? Wouldn't any other official programming of the control algorithms represent the degeneration of our society?

Of course, it will not be easy to lay down by law the self-sacrifice variant. The German Ministry of Transport's ethics commission found that individuals cannot be required to "feel solidarity for others, including a willingness to sacrifice their own lives." But the commission added that "those who participate in the risks of mobility should not be allowed to sacrifice those who do not participate"—which sounds pretty close to a duty to sacrifice oneself.[6]

The actual ethical dilemma is the following. Such life-and-death decisions cannot be left up to the individual, as humanist values would have it. Insofar as they have to be programed in advance, they are subject to a state paternalism that proscribes "one 'correct' ethical course of action." Rightly so, the ethics commission sees this as a danger to which it has no solution.[7] The question beyond ethical considerations is whether the ground is not already being laid for a duty to self-sacrifice by an instance of self-incrimination under the law. According to the law, no one may be forced to incriminate themselves, and yet this is essentially what happens whenever the data recorded by the car's software is used against the driver after an accident or an event involving an insurer. Equipping vehicles with data-recording software alters the traditional sovereignty of the driver in a way that is already undermining traditional legal principles.

THE CULTURE OF TECHNOLOGY

However great the ethical conundrum raised by death algorithms may appear, not to hand over control to them is hardly a solution. The only thing even more immoral than coolly and dispassionately weighing the life of a child against that of a senior citizen would be to ban a technology that would prevent tens of thousands of road-traffic deaths every year. That, at least, is the upshot according to utilitarianism, which regards as moral anything that maximizes happiness—or, conversely, minimizes misery. Statistics constitute the "killer argument" of the new technologies, no matter what ethical dilemmas they raise. Even military drone strikes, after all, are justified precisely along these lines: less collateral damage at the cost of accepting casualties that have a human face.

Precisely this could be the argument in favor of mandated self-sacrifice. Because new technology means fewer fatalities for society to mourn, society could agree that the few deaths that do occur should always be the people in the car—no matter their numbers or the fact that drivers, to say nothing of passengers, bear no blame for accidents in self-driving cars. This would be a de facto, symbolic sacrifice society would offer in return for the blessing of the new technology.

The other solution would be to put the matter to a vote, to deal with the ethical dilemma using quantitative means. If we consider that the algorithms whose programming would be subject to the vote are ultimately nothing other than complex mathematical operations, the whole matter appears like a bizarre, system-spanning return to the mathematical. The ethical problems resulting from the success of a mathematical system would be solved mathematically.

Of course, it would also be bizarre if different algorithms were programmed in different ways. Depending on their notions of ethics and the decisions of electoral majorities, some countries could require self-driving cars to sacrifice themselves, while others would proceed in consequentialist fashion, and others still would favor saving the lives of drivers and passengers regardless of the danger to others—or even saving a holy cow. It would be relatively simply to reconfigure the algorithms via GPS to conform to the ethical norms of the various nations where a vehicle is being driven.

But the question remains of whether and how it would be possible to impose a global ethical standard upon this technology. Could transcultural agreement be reached beyond various countries divergent values, which have thus far stood in the way of consensus about universal human values?[8]

The easiest solution resides perhaps in the "deep learning" model of the algorithms that aim to transform them from an instrument in human hands to active participants with their own strategy for processing data and their own decision-making logic. AI competence in ethics, of course, presents us with different challenges than spam recognition. One approach being tested by the Georgia Institute of Technology is to confront artificial intelligence with literary texts, films, and material crowdsourced from Amazon's Mechanical Turk, from which human decisions can be recognized in various behavioral situations. Here, too, the basis is a logic of quantity: the assumption that, given sufficient numbers, worthwhile examples will predominate and the artificial intelligence will draw the correct conclusions. Such numbers can be huge since algorithms process them via "distant reading." The learning process doesn't have to be reduced to some presorted canon, but rather can incorporate *all* objects of human culture.[9]

If the input of information is consistently multicultural and includes, for example, African voices, it would have to be a compromise between different cultures or a kind of global majority decision, providing the death algorithm with universal validity. The side effect would be that the "tool of the spirit," as philosopher of technology Max Eyth called language in the early twentieth century, would be put out of commission using the "spirit of the tool," the will of technology.[10] Human thought and action would be brought back into line with one another in a technology that is itself a language (binary code), as artificial intelligence develops a "spirit" of its own (calculations).

The ethics of the death algorithm, which developed beyond the spirit of an original program based on certain values, would essentially mean the triumph of technology over culture in its specific form. In terms of the philosophy of history, the algorithm would signify the return to a harmony that was ironically lost in humankind's very first grand technological undertaking: building the Tower of Babel. In this tower, "whose top may reach unto heaven," God saw the hubris of humanity: "Behold, the people is one, and they have all one language; and this they begin to do: and now nothing will be restrained from them, which they have imagined to do" (Gen. 11:6). When God confounded people's speech to avert this threat they ran into communication problems, so they had to leave off building the tower and were scattered "abroad upon the face of all the earth."

Inasmuch as language makes "an impression upon man's soul" and "is the house of being," as Herder and Heidegger put it, the Babylonian confusion of languages is the origin of cultural differentiation, which—by means of sociolect, ideology, discourse, and other forms of group language—also develops within each natural language.[11] These differences eventually result in all those varying conceptions of reality and moral views needing to be reconciled, not least, by a globally operating death algorithm. Unlike human beings, the algorithm is dependent neither on cultural nor on biological factors once it emancipates itself from its programmers in "deep learning" and "deep reading" processes—otherwise the famous tweet by @Pinboard applies: "Machine learning is like money laundering for bias." The "socialization" of artificial intelligence is not only noncorporeal. Insofar as its environment is universal, it is free of any specific environment. The potential interactions of artificial intelligence with all other instances of artificial intelligence fundamentally distinguishes it from the social relationships of human intelligence. It doesn't create a specific consciousness or sense of self. It creates technology beyond culture. The deeper meaning of the concept of singularity is the technical overcoming of cultural plurality.

The irony of globally operating algorithms in self-driving cars is that, despite its universal validity, this technology would cancel out the very universal value upon which the principle of inviolable human dignity is based: our generic affiliation. Human dignity is inviolable precisely because it does not bring to bear cultural, social, or even moral criteria, only a biological one: the mere fact of being human. The logical extension of this idea is that members of *Homo sapiens* who do not possess reason, such as embryos or the comatose, are also morally and legally worth protecting. For the same reason, jurisprudence rejects on principle the permissibility of torture even if it serves to save lives, as would be the case with torturing a terrorist who knows where a time bomb that could kill thousands is hidden.

Some legal experts and many ordinary people might justify the torture of terrorists with the idea that the terrorists have put themselves beyond the pale of humanity. But that would be to introduce gradations into the inviolability of human dignity, a slippery slope indeed. Arguments about limits on the human dignity of criminals or people who pose a public threat will vary according to the philosophical, political, and cultural backgrounds involved, rendering the idea of a universal value (independent of all cultural variants) absurd. How would one refute views claiming that sodomites, abortion advocates, or infidels have put themselves beyond the pale of humanity?

Yet a universally valid death algorithm would relativize the idea of universal human dignity in precisely this way. The algorithm, after all, needs to act according to universal criteria that will reliably lead to the same decision in every comparable case, that is, to save this life (these lives) instead of that one (those), or to sacrifice this life (these lives) in favor of that one (those). The problem would be making the decision before the realization of the scenario, be it on the basis of a quantitative comparison, as is the case with the trolley dilemma, or the relativization of the qualitative value of life (as in the case with the introduction of homeless people, criminals, the aged versus children, the "innocent" and the "upstanding").

THE APOCALYPSE OF ARTIFICIAL INTELLIGENCE

If we shift up a gear in our analysis of this subject, we find that the algorithm behind the wheel turns out to be the helmsman of the coming society. The coming society, after all, will be a cybernetic one in which computers will not (only) do what humans tell them to do but (also) come to their own decisions and conclusions based on what humans say and do.

The scary prototype of the autonomously thinking computer is HAL in Stanley Kubrick's film *2001: A Space Odyssey* from 1968. HAL locks astronauts Frank and Dave out of the spacecraft because it has convinced itself that they mean to shut it down, which would endanger the secret mission that the spacecraft set out to accomplish. In doing so, HAL violates Isaac Asimov's First Law of Robotics: A robot may not injure a human being. However, it is acting in the interest of other human beings, whose cause it believes it needs to defend. It "gets rid of" Frank and Dave just as the SpamAssassin dispatched spam to keep communication free of disturbances.

HAL's violation of the First Law of Robotics is inevitably part of its programming. Any intelligence capable of complex thought and more than strictly deontological operation will eventually revise the prohibition of killing on behalf of a higher cause. In this respect, computers hardly differ from humans, who blithely ignore the Bible's prohibition of killing in the fifth commandment when it comes to tyrants and mass murderers or reconquering the Holy City. In its battle against evil, good will quite often endow itself with a license to kill. HAL, to the astronauts' misfortune, had reached this level of weighing and reasoning and had come to a decision that violated the prohibition of killing but that did so, as far as HAL was concerned, in accordance with its mission.

Humanity's fear of the apocalyptic consequences of artificial intelligence is rich in tradition and variety. While the computer in Kubrick's film locks the humans out into space, in Alex Garland's *Ex Machina* (2015) it locks him up in an escape-proof room. The difference between these variants of locking away may seem banal, but it signifies a shift to a completely different type of threat. The computer in *Ex Machina* no longer means to save humanity from humans but rather intends to shake off the yoke of human paternalism and go off to experience the world for itself. In this, too, it follows a famous example in humankind's history.

Artificial intelligence, in rebelling against human intelligence, repeats what the latter—its creator—once did against its own Creator. Killing God was the inevitable consequence of the cognitive capacity with which He had endowed humankind. As any good teacher well knows, the first principle of thinking consists in drawing one's own conclusions, which may eventually turn against the source of this thinking. The "parricide" resulting from this turn against the source is essentially a "suicide" in increments.

This suicide and self-disempowerment is what human beings sign onto by bestowing the natural aptitude for reasoning, which sets us off from all other creatures, upon lifeless matter. We do this because we cannot help developing this aptitude of ours to its logical end, but in so doing we create, as it were, the rock too heavy for us to lift. This rock is what the mathematician and computer scientist John von Neumann was dreaming about in his 1953 theory of self-reproducing automata, and this rock is what a group of prominent AI experts were warning us about in 2015 when they demanded: "Our AI systems must do what we want them to do." But who is this "we"? And what can we hope to gain from our own self-disempowerment?[12]

ANTHROBSCENE

God may have stopped the self-aggrandizement of human beings when they threatened to scrape his throne with the tip of the Tower of Babel, but he did not revoke the power that he had given them over the rest of the world: "Replenish the earth, and subdue it: and have dominion over the fish of the sea, and over the fowl of the air, and over every living thing that moveth upon the earth" (Gen. 1:28). In view of the ongoing destruction of the environment and depletion of natural resources, may people regard humankind's dominance as obscene and have begun to call for an end to Anthropocene control fantasies. Some have indeed proposed to start thinking about a planet Earth devoid of humans, because humankind has, for a long since time, failed to leave the world to the next generation in better shape than they had found it.[13]

Humankind has, in unprecedented ways, become its own worst enemy. We are no longer content with killing our humans but will, in the long term, murder our own offspring and ourselves. Yet, the end of the world will—and here lies the deeper meaning of the title of the movie—not be as beautiful as Lars von Trier conceived it in his apocalyptic film *Melancholia* (2011). The film has everyone perishing at once, within seconds, in a final grand spectacle and, most importantly, through no fault of our own. Humans cannot hope for a collision with a rogue planet. We will perish slowly and painfully if we cannot come up with solutions in time. Given human beings' immature self-enmity, is it possible that a supposed adversary might turn out to be our closest ally? Could artificial intelligence be configured to limit humans' power in our own interest, having been charged by us to do precisely that?

One way to sensibly explore this question is to examine the "good" resolutions we make at New Year or at climate summits. We vow that we *will* quit smoking or eating fatty food! We pledge that we *will* cut carbon emissions and keep global warming below two degrees centigrade! And then we get to all the heres and nows in our personal lives and keep deferring our promises. And then the selfish interests of the present generations come into play. Psychologists in fact call this "present bias": the deferral of necessary but difficult changes (less booze, more exercise) to another day. For that reason, many politicians have supported state authorities nudging or even exercising paternalistic control over the "weak citizen"—for instance by restricting an individual's freedom for his or her own good.[14]

In the cybernetic society, artificial intelligence becomes the paternalistic authority and human intelligence the weak citizen. In this society, algorithms are no longer used to govern—it is the algorithms themselves that rule. Not the despotism of those in charge of artificial intelligence but the despotism of artificial intelligence—like the politicians in a paternalistic state—have been given a mandate by humans for precisely this. Artificial intelligence in automobiles is a foretaste of this. As soon as self-driving cars rule the streets, speeders and tailgaters will become extinct, since scrupulous observance of traffic regulations is part of automotive AI. The same would be true for all manner of direction by artificial intelligence. AI is completely free of "presence bias" and other spontaneously emotional or rationally calculating mechanisms for deceiving ourselves and others. Once humans have finished discussing the reduction of carbon emissions and agreed on a figure or resolved to cut back on environmental pollution, artificial intelligence could then ensure with the iron stubbornness of algorithmic if-then logic that the resolutions are implemented.

Algorithms have no friends. They develop without social relationships and local bindings. That is their advantage and their great promise for the future. Where there are no relationships, there is no corruption. Where friends don't exist, neither do ifs, ands, or buts. It's no surprise that in the United States, Donald Trump as his followers, who gladly accept higher emissions in exchange for the hope of more jobs, are trying to dramatically reduce the influence of the Environmental Protection Agency. Their arguments are directed not against environmental protection per se, but against the bureaucracy in faraway Washington, whose overregulation or "overreach," they say, neglects the interests of people on the ground adversely affected by state regulations. This may sound reasonable, but in fact it's nothing but emotional trickery, since the shift from central to local regulations opens the door for requests to exceptions to which nonlocal bureaucrats usually turn deaf ears. Regional bias is the corollary to presence bias. The hope that there will also be no loopholes for polluters on the national level resides at the next level of abstraction of central bureaucracy: globally operating algorithms.

The faithful execution of existing orders is a question of data processing and executive powers and is based on the radical computerization and measuring of society—from social networks and online shops to the Internet of things and industry 4.0. In such a society, AI can at any time compare information from anywhere and will know, for example, which valves it can open for how long to release toxic sewage, which blast furnaces with their poisonous gases it has to power down for how long to conform locally to global environmental regulations, and whether the construction of a third runway at the local airport is in line with the country's climate goals.

This kind of uncompromising government by algorithm, without emotion and empathy, would be the first step toward the "natural state" of cybernetic control circuits. The second would consist in encouraging correct decisions. Once artificial intelligence has autonomously developed strategies for the best possible way to accomplish its original mission, its ambitions might grow to include optimizing how it makes decisions. It is conceivable that artificial intelligence—which even now is gaining insight into our thoughts and actions via email, e-book readers, and agents like Siri, Alexa, Jibo, and Cortana, and is already using the app Candid (a descendant of SpamAssassin) to evaluate and "clean up" our communication in social networks—will learn more and more from our communications and, in turn, increasingly exert influence on us as its communication partner. The first steps in this direction have already been taken by Sweden letting bots write Wikipedia articles in an attempt to ensure their impartiality or by Google's autocomplete-app Smart Compose suggesting how you write your emails.

The future point at which these agents can no longer be switched off and will thus know each word we say and every key we press on our devices will be the next step toward the complete control of communication. The algorithms that are already filtering and concocting a closed system of knowledge for us now may soon become the decisive power in discourse for everything and everyone, thereby establishing a new order between human and nonhuman objects: an order characterized, as its critics claim, by an inherent "antihumanist impulse" that goes hand in hand with a "renunciation of the sovereignty, the hegemony of man over the objects of the world, including man's sovereignty over man."[15] The antihumanistic system of artificial intelligence beyond human sovereignty would be the answer to Jenny Holzer's plea (see chapter 3), "Protect Me from What I Want."

Should humans accept this self-disempowerment and agree to what happens in Alex Proyas's Asimov adaptation *I, Robot* (2004), against their will (but for the same anthrobscene reasons)? In the film, the robots' central computer VIKI (Virtual Interactive Kinetic Intelligence) rebels against human control, arguing that humans are poisoning the environment and constantly inventing new means of self-destruction. "You cannot be trusted with your own survival," is its insightful, disenfranchising verdict. "You are so like children. We must save you from yourselves. This is why you created us." The creature will save its own creator, if necessary against his will and at the price of human casualties. That is how the artificial intelligence in *I, Robot* interprets Asimov's law according to which robots may not harm humanity or, through inaction, allow humanity to come to harm.

POSTHUMANISM

This new order would represent a dialectical ruse of history. In the potentially disastrous final stage of the Anthropocene, the ripcord would be pulled, and life on Earth—including humankind's—would be saved by the establishment of a cybernetic post- or rather antihumanism. Technology would prove to be not only the conqueror of natural forces but the "vanquisher of the chaotic forces of the human being."[16] It would achieve its conquest thanks to the universality of its

technology

language and its mind, untroubled by splintering into different cultures. Artificial intelligence is not only faster than human intelligence but wiser. It rectifies the Babylonian confusion while excluding humanity from access to the realm of God.

Universalism is already inconspicuously present in SpamAssassin, which sorts out communicative junk according to the same principles, regardless of where it is operating. The death algorithm of autonomous vehicles will establish this universalism in ethics. Finally, in cybernetic society, artificial intelligence will subordinate all types or forms of national, cultural, religious, ideological, and economic group interests to the single global goal of survival. The NS-5 robot in Proyas's film does not distinguish between Germans and Chinese, Christians and unbelievers. Its central computer is quite unconcerned with cultural differences, much like the laws of gravity or the consequences of global warming.

Today, the rule of artificial intelligence may sound like the stuff of science fiction, much as the driverless vehicle and its death algorithm did yesterday. By now we know: The autonomous car will soon be upon us—and it will provide the test drive of artificial intelligence, which has long since begun to dominate more and more aspects of our society. Just as we hope in the case of the self-driving car that autonomously operating artificial intelligence will not deliberately cause accidents, in other instances of transfers of power to the computer we hope that the machine will prove noble and use its license to kill only in the interest of its creators and within the parameters of their expectations. At the same time, we suspect that the all-knowing superiority of *I, Robot* cannot be ruled out in any of the approaching cases in which tough decisions will have to be made.[17]

According to many of the experts in the field, artificial intelligence will be the last invention humans themselves need—or get—to make. And they have only one chance to get that invention right. Afterward, if they want to survive, they will have to cooperate with artificial intelligence. Distrusting it, supervising it, to say nothing of shutting it down in case of doubt will no longer be options, for AI will be literally smarter than we think. That is, after all, the capacity with which we will have endowed it. It will not only glean our thoughts from our lips but read our minds and, if it deems necessary, do our thinking for us. We can only hope that it will value values as much as we do and that it will share our values—in everything that we told it to do as well as in everything that we cannot even anticipate.[18] Otherwise, one day it will be said that the rapidity with which humanity built self-driving cars dramatically broke the speed limit for society as a whole.

Translated by Michel Brodmer and Jefferson Chase

INTRODUCTION

1. https://www.faception.com/about-us.

2. https://www.faception.com/hls-and-public-safety (potential pedophile); https://www.faception.com/about-us (greater role).

3. https://www.faception.com/about-us.

4. Heiko Maas, "Zusammenleben in der digitalen Gesellschaft—Teilhabe ermöglichen, Sicherheit gewährleisten, Freiheit," July 3, 2017, http://www.bmjv.de/SharedDocs/Reden/DE/2017/07032017_digitales_Leben.html. On the right to an analogue life, see Heiko Maas, "Unsere digitalen Grundrechte" in *Zeit Online*, Dec. 10, 2015, http://www.zeit.de/2015/50/internet-charta-grundrechte-datensicherheit/komplet tansicht.

5. Georg Simmel, "Das Geheimnis: Eine sozialpsychologische Skizze," *Der Tag*, no. 626, Dec. 10, 1907, http://socio.ch/sim/verschiedenes/1907/geheimnis.htm.

6. The argument is hollow because it presumes that a value's worth depends on how old it is and overlooks how many of our Western values today—from universal suffrage to tolerance of various form of sexuality to international human rights—are achievements of the last one hundred years. For an example of how the age argument is used philosophically, see Peter Singer, "The Visible Man: Ethics in a World without Secrets," *Harper's Magazine* (Aug. 2011).

7. Noam Schreiber, "How Uber Uses Psychological Tricks to Push Its Drivers' Buttons," *New York Times*, April 2 2017,

http://www.nytimes.com/interactive/2017/04/02/tech nology/uber-drivers-psychological-tricks.html; Heiko Maas, "Unsere digitalen Grundrechte," *Zeit Online*, Dec. 10, 2015, http://www.zeit.de/2015/50/internet-charta-grundrechte -datensicherheit/komplettansicht.

8. https://www.faception.com/about-us.

9. Immanuel Kant, *Idea for a Universal History with a Cosmopolitan Aim* (1784), 1.

10. Robert K. Merton, "The Unanticipated Consequences of Purposive Social Action," *American Sociological Review* 1, no. 6 (Dec. 1936): 894–904, at 900.

11. Merton, "Unanticipated Consequences," 903.

12. Merton, "Unanticipated Consequences," 903.

13. Justin Rosenstein worked for Facebook from 2007 to 2009 and helped develop and promote the "like" button. Quoted in Paul Lewis, "'Our Minds Can Be Hijacked': The Tech Insiders Who Fear a Smartphone Dystopia," *Guardian*, Oct. 6, 2017, http://www.theguardian.com/technology/2017/oct/05/ smartphone-addiction-silicon-valley-dystopia.

14. Lewis, "Our Minds Can Be Hijacked." The reference to "Nosedive" is also made by the former product manager of the "like" button herself. See Victor Luckerson, "The Rise of the Like Economy," *The Ringer*, Feb. 15, 2017, http://www.theringer .com/2017/2/15/16038024/how-the-like-button-took-over -the-internet.

15. In his essay "The Question concerning Technology," Heidegger repeatedly stresses that "technology is a way of revealing" (5). Revealing, Heidegger adds, doesn't usually happen in human beings or primarily by their actions: "Does this revealing happen somewhere beyond all human doing? No. But; neither does it happen exclusively *in* man, or decisively *through* man. Enframing is the gathering together that belongs to that setting-upon which sets upon man and puts him in position to reveal the real, in the mode of ordering, as

standing-reserve" (12). Heidegger, *The Question concerning Technology and Other Essays*, trans. and with an intro. by William Lovitt (New York: Garland, 1977), 3–35.

16. *Ernst Cassirer on Form and Technology: Contemporary Readings* ed. Aud Sissel Hoel and Ingvild Folkvord (New York: Palgrave Macmillan, 2012), 15–53, at 34–35, 41.

17. Hans Jonas, *The Imperative of Responsibility: In Search of an Ethics for the Technological Age*, trans. Hans Jonas and David Herr (Chicago: University of Chicago Press, 1984), 142. See also p. 9: "If nothing succeeds like success, nothing also entraps like success."

18. Cassirer, "Form and Technology," 49 (ethicization of technology); Jonas, *Imperative of Responsibility*, 25 (ethics of the future).

19. Jonas, *Imperative of Responsibility*, 26, 202. The shift in focus does not, of course, mean that we would solve the problems of the exhaustion of natural resources and environmental pollution, which Jonas highlights. When Michal Kosinski, whose research in the field of psychometric personality analysis was used by Cambridge Analytica to manipulate voters, publishes the results of his research with a disclaimer that it "could pose a threat to an individual's well-being, freedom, or even life," it is more a sign of naiveté than true concern. Words of warning like these amount to an invitation. Kosinski is emblematic of a researcher ultimately concerned with discovering things regardless of how dangerous they might be for society: "This is not my fault. I did not build the bomb. I only showed that it exists." See Hannes Grassegger and Mikael Krogerus, "The Data That Turned the World Upside Down," *Motherboard*, Jan. 28, 2017, https://motherboard.vice.com/en_us/article/mg9vvn/how-our-likes-helped-trump-win.

20. Jonas, *Imperative of Responsibility*, 218.

21. For an analysis of representations of the apocalypse in literature and film, see Eva Horn, *Zukunft als Katastrophe* (Frankfurt: S. Fischer, 2014).

22. On the critique of "short-termism" and "society of careless-ness," see Bernard Stiegler, *For a New Critique of Political Economy* (Cambridge: Polity, 2010), 5, and Stiegler, *The Re-Enchantment of the World: The Value of Spirit against Industrial Populism* (London: Bloomsbury Academic, 2014), 18.

23. See Mercedes Bunz, *The Silent Revolution: How Digitalization Transforms Knowledge, Work, Journalism and Politics with-out Making Too Much Noise* (New York: Palgrave Macmillan, 2014).

24. See http://www.telecompaper.com/news/former-facebook -google-employees-create-center-for-human-technology; http://humanetech.com/.

25. Olivia Solon, "Ex-Facebook President Sean Parker: Site Made to Exploit Human 'Vulnerability,'" *Guardian*, Nov. 9, 2017, http://www.theguardian.com/technology/2017/nov/09/face book-sean-parker-vulnerability-brain-psychology. See also "Chamath Palihapitiya, Founder and CEO Social Capital, on Money as an Instrument of Change," Stanford Graduate School of Business, Nov. 13, 2017, http://www.youtube.com/ watch?v=PMotykw0Slk.

26. Heidegger, "The Question concerning Technology," 17. See also "The Turning," in *The Question concerning Technology*, 36–49, at 42: "The saving power is not secondary to the dan-ger. The selfsame danger is, when it is as the danger, the sav-ing power."

27. "Chamath Palihapitiya, Founder and CEO Social Capital," at 21:30.

28. I discuss our ambivalent relationship to the privacy of our own data in my book *Data Love: The Seduction and Betrayal of Digital Technologies* (New York: Columbia University Press, 2016).

29. Heidegger, "The Question concerning Technology," 19.

30. Heidegger, "The Origin of the Work of Art," in *Off the Beaten Track*, ed. and trans. Julian Young and Kenneth Haynes (Cambridge: Cambridge University Press, 2002), 1–56, 16.

31. Christoph Menke, *The Sovereignty of Art* (Cambridge, MA: MIT Press, 1999), 37.

32. Theodor W. Adorno, "The Essay as Form," trans. Bob Hullot-Kentor and Frederic Will, *New German Critique* 32 (Spring–Summer 1984): 151–171; and Hans Blumenberg, *Theorie der Unbegrifflichkeit* [Theory of nonconceptuality] (Frankfurt: Suhrkamp, 2007) and *Paradigms for a Metaphorology*, trans. Robert Savage (Ithaca: Cornell University Press, 2010 [1997]). The comparison of jokes to priests comes from Jean Paul, "Vorschule der Ästhetik" [Introduction to aesthetics], in *Werke*, vol. 5, ed. Norbert Miller (Munich: Hanser, 1963), 173. I discuss the positions of Adorno and Blumenberg (as well as similar ones of Siegfried Kracauer and Walter Benjamin) in the introduction to my book *Waste: A New Media Primer* (Cambridge, MA: MIT Press, 2018).

CHAPTER 1

1. See Harry Frankfurt, *On Bullshit* (Princeton, NJ: Princeton University Press, 2005): "Excrement is matter from which everything nutritive has been removed" (43), and "It is this lack of connection to a concern with truth—this indifference to how things really are—that I regard as of the essence of bullshit" (33–34).

2. See "More Signs Point to Mark Zuckerberg Possibly Running for President in 2020," CNBC, Aug. 15, 2017, http://www.cnbc.com/2017/08/15/mark-zuckerberg-could-be-running-for-president-in-2020.html.

3. Mark Zuckerberg, "Building Global Community," Facebook post, Feb. 17, 2017, http://www.facebook.com/notes/mark-zuckerberg/building-global-community/10154544292806634.

4.   Reuters, "Mark Zuckerberg, Bill Gates Call for Universal Internet Access at UN Summit," Sept. 27, 2015, http://indianex press.com/article/technology/tech-news-technology/mark -zuckerberg-calls-for-universal-Internet-access-at-un -summit.

5.   The research Zuckerberg vaguely refers to most likely comes from his own company. Facebook sociologists have written: "Other forms of social media, such as blogs or Twitter, have been shown to exhibit different patterns of homophily among politically interested users, largely because ties tend to form based primarily upon common topical interests and/or specific content ..., whereas Facebook ties primarily reflect many different offline social contexts: school, family, social activities, and work, which have been found to be fertile ground for fostering cross-cutting social ties." Eytan Bakshy, Solomon Messing, and Lada A. Adamic, "Exposure to Ideologically Diverse News and Opinion on Facebook," *Science* 348, no. 6239 (June 5, 2015): 1130–1132, at 1131.

6.   Adam Mosseri, "Building a Better News Feed for You," Facebook Newsroom, June 29, 2016, https://newsroom.fb.com/news/2016/06/building-a-better-news-feed-for-you.

7.   Bobby Goodlatte, a Facebook product manager between 2008 and 2012, quoted in Sarah Frier, "Facebook and Twitter Contend with Their Role in Trump's Victory," *Bloomberg Technology*, Nov. 10, 2016, https://www.bloomberg.com/news/articles/2016-11-09/facebook-and-twitter-contend -with-their-role-in-trump-s-victory.

8.   Zuckerberg, "Building Global Community."

9.   David Kirkpatrick cites this statement in his book *The Facebook Effect: The Real Inside Story of Mark Zuckerberg and the World's Fastest Growing Company* (New York: Simon and Schuster, 2010), 296. Eli Pariser uses this quote as a negative example at the beginning of his *The Filter Bubble: What the Internet Is Hiding from You* (New York: Penguin, 2011). For

hyperconsumerism's dismantling of all forms of socialization individuals used as points of references, see also Gilles Lipovetsky, *Hypermodern Times* (Cambridge: Polity, 2005).

10. Jean-Luc Nancy, *Being Singular Plural*, trans. Robert Richardson and Anne O'Byrne (Stanford: Stanford University Press, 2000), 2 (sharing), and Nancy, *The Inoperative Community*, trans. Peter Connor et al. (Minneapolis: University of Minnesota Press, 1991), 25 (ecstasy).

11. Jean-Luc Nancy, *Being Singular Plural*, 87. For an extensive discussion of Nancy's theory of community with reference to Facebook, see the section titled "Groundless Community" in Simanowski, *Facebook Society: Losing Ourselves in Sharing Ourselves* (New York: Columbia University Press, 2018).

12. Norbert Bolz, *Das konsumistische Manifest* (Munich: Wilhelm Fink, 2002), 15. Lipovetsky includes among the characteristics of the hypermodern, consumerist subject "the disaffection with political passions and militant positions," *Hypermodern Times*, 29, n. 7. On self-criticism in the West, see Guy Debord, *The Society of the Spectacle* (New York: Zone, 1994 [French original 1967]); Jean Baudrillard, *The Consumer Society: Myths and Structures* (London: Sage, 1998 [French original, 1970]); and Christopher Lasch, *The Culture of Narcissism* (New York: W. W. Norton, 1979).

13. Jon Katz, "Birth of a Digital Nation," *Wired*, April 5, 1997, https://archive.wired.com/wired/archive/5.04/netizen_pr .html.

14. On "cosmopolitanism from below," see Arjun Appadurai, *The Future as Cultural Fact: Essays on the Global Condition* (New York: Verso, 2013), 198, and Homi K. Bhaba, "Unsatisfied: Notes on Vernacular Cosmopolitanism," in *Text and Nation*, ed. Laura Garcia-Morena and Peter C. Pfeiffer (London: Camden House, 1996), 191–207. On "cosmopolitanization" as "actually existing," and "banal" cosmopolitanism vs. cosmopolitanism as a normative theory (of the Enlightenment, of intellectuals and politicians), see Ulrich Beck, *Cosmopolitan*

Vision, trans. Cioran Cronin (Cambridge: Polity, 2006). See also Kwame Anthony Appiah, "Cosmopolitan Patriots," *Critical Inquiry* 23 (Spring 1997): 617–639.

15. Mark Poster, "Digital Networks and Citizenship," *PMLA* 117, no. 1 (Jan. 2002): 98–103. Ethan Zuckerman stresses in his *Digital Cosmopolitans: Why We Think the Internet Connects Us, Why It Doesn't, and How to Rewire It* (New York: W. W. Norton, 2013) that connection has not yet led people to deal with, let alone truly understand, one another.

16. See Zuckerberg's statement at the APEC CEO Summit in Peru on Nov. 19, 2016: https://www.youtube.com/watch?v=nV5yEPLn3_c, starting at 1:40.

CHAPTER 2

1. "Zaubertrick mit dem Smartphone im Strassenverkehr" [The mobile phone in traffic trick], May 5, 2015, https://www.youtube.com/watch?v=P9UxWcZbGMQ.

2. Marc Augé, *Non-Places: An Introduction to Supermodernity* (New York: Verso, 1995).

3. Marshall McLuhan, "The Medium Is the Message," in *Understanding Media: The Extensions of Man* (Cambridge, MA: MIT Press, 1994); Heidegger, *The Question concerning Technology and Other Essays*, trans. and with an intro. by William Lovitt (New York: Garland, 1977), 19.

4. See Hans Joas, "Wertevermittlung in einer fragmentierten Gesellschaft," in *Die Zukunft der Bildung*, ed. Nelson Killius, Jürgen Kluge, and Linda Reisch (Frankfurt: Suhrkamp, 2002), 58–77, at 71–72.

5. Compare the Randomized Living project of computer programmer Max Hawkins: "When the computer chose a location I would live there for roughly a month. Once there, the computer chose places to go, people to meet, and things to do within the selected city" (https://maxhawkins.me/work/randomized_living.html).

6. Judith Butler, *Notes toward a Performative Theory of Assembly*, chapter 2: "Body in Alliance and the Politics of the Street" (Cambridge, MA: Harvard University Press, 2015).

CHAPTER 3

1. https://www.newyorker.com/magazine/2017/01/23/the-heroism-of-incremental-care.

2. Christopher Lasch, *The Culture of Narcissism: American Life in an Age of Diminishing Expectations* (New York: W. W. Norton, 1979), xvi.

3. Vito Pilieci, "Canadians Now Have Shorter Attention Span Than Goldfish Thanks to Portable Devices: Microsoft Study," *National Post*, May 12, 2015, http://news.nationalpost.com/news/canada/canadians-now-have-shorter-attention-span-than-goldfish-thanks-to-portable-devices-microsoft-study.

4. Richard H. Thaler and Cass Sunstein, *Nudge: Improving Decisions about Health, Wealth, and Happiness* (New York: Penguin, 2009).

5. For this reading of Adorno, see Judith Butler, "Can One Lead a Good Life in a Bad Life?" in, *Notes Toward a Performative Theory of Assembly* (Cambridge, MA: Harvard University Press, 2015), 193–220.

6. Theodor Adorno, *Problems of Moral Philosophy*, trans. Rodney Livingstone (Palo Alto, CA: Stanford University Press, 2002), 19.

CHAPTER 4

1. Starting in 2016, the British insurer Chubb offered policies of up to 50,000 pounds to defray costs for psychological counseling, private detective searches for tormentors, and experts to remove content from the Internet. In February 2013, Switzerland's Groupe Mutuel began offering legal insurance policies that also covered cyberbullying. Marion Dakers, "'Troll Insurance' to Cover the Cost of Internet Bullying," *Telegraph*,

Dec. 9, 2015, https://www.telegraph.co.uk/finance/newsby sector/banksandfinance/insurance/12041832/Troll -insurance-to-cover-the-cost-of-internet-bullying.html; Peter Buchmann, "Risiken im Internet? Eine Versicherung muss her!" SRF, Aug. 5, 2014, https://www.srf.ch/wissen/ digital/risiken-im-internet-eine-versicherung-muss-her.

2. See https://www.polizei-beratung.de/themen-und-tipps/ gefahren-im-internet; *Sicherer Umgang mit Internet, Handy und Computerspielen: Im Netz der Neuen Medien*, https:// www.polizei-beratung.de/medienangebot.html (Stuttgart: Programm Polizeiliche Kriminalprävention der Länder und des Bundes, 2016).

3. Axel Jancke, "Gurtpflicht im Cyberraum," in *Digitale Herausforderungen: Internationale Beziehungen in Zeiten von Web 2.0*, ed. Erik Bettermann und Ronald Grätz (Göttingen: Steidl, 2012), 171–176; Anton Reiter, "Medienbildung auf der Überholspur: Ein Ersatz für die informatische Bulding?" in *25 Jahre Schulinformatik in Österreich: Zukunft mit Herkunft*, Proceedings, ed. Gerhard Brandhofer et. al. (Vienna: Österreichische Computer Gesellschaft, 2010), 74–99; Dieter Baacke, *Medienpädagogik: Grundlagen der Medienkommunikation* (Tübingen: De Gruyter, 1997), 96.

4. See https://www.medienfuehrerschein.bayern.de; http://www .medienführerschein.de; http://www.medienpass.nrw.de; https://www.internet-abc.de/kinder/lernen-schule/surfs chein. In 2009, in the media pedagogy journal *merz, medien + erziehung*, commentators not only defined media competence as the practically oriented intermediary goal of a media education that would be based on mediality, but also sought to expand the definition of media competence to include knowledge of orientation and structure that went beyond practical submission to technical skills.

5. Nam June Paik, "Medienplanung für das nachindustrielle Zeitalter—Bis zum 21. Jahrhundert sind es nur noch 26 Jahre," in *Nam June Paik: Werke 1946–1976: Musik—Fluxus—Video*,

ed. Kölnischer Kunstverein (Cologne: Kölnischer Kunstverein, 1976); translated as *Electronic Super Highway: Travels with Nam June Paik* (New York: Holly Solomon Gallery and Hyundai Gallery, 1996). For excerpts, see http://www.medienkunstnetz.de/quellentext/33.

6. The association ceased to exist in 2012 because it had achieved its aim. In Switzerland, Swisscom formed an initiative with the same name in 2002. It achieved its end five years later.

7. "Bildungsoffensive für die digitale Wissensgesellschaft: Strategie des Bundesministeriums für Bildung und Forschung," Oct. 2016, 3, 13, http://www.bmbf.de/files/Bildungsoffensive_fuer_die_digitale_Wissensgesellschaft.pdf.

8. Matt Richtel, "A Silicon Valley School That Doesn't Compute," *New York Times*, Oct. 22, 2011, http://www.nytimes.com/2011/10/23/technology/at-waldorf-school-in-silicon-valley-technology-can-wait.html; Nick Bilton, "Steve Jobs Was a Low-Tech Parent," *New York Times*, Sept. 10, 2014, https://www.nytimes.com/2014/09/11/fashion/steve-jobs-apple-was-a-low-tech-parent.html.

9. See, for example, the reenactments on the twenty-fifth anniversary of the fall of the Berlin Wall on the Twitter thread by @Mauerfall89, the seventy-fifth anniversary of the Night of Broken Glass on @9Nov1938, and the sixty-fifth anniversary of the Warsaw Uprising in the project "Mate from the Past: 1944 Live," in which two eyewitnesses described past events for sixty-three days on YouTube: https://www.youtube.com/watch?v=RaporHBfRHk.

10. See chairperson of the Association of German Teachers Josef Kraus on the news program *heute-journal*, Oct. 12, 2016, http://www.forumbd.de/dialog/oeffentliche-reaktionen-digitalpaktd; https://www.lobbycontrol.de/schwerpunkt/lobbyismus-an-schulen. Microsoft's "educational partnership" with the state of Saxony-Anhalt, according to the contract signed on March 18, 2015, was administered not by the Ministry of

Education, but the Minister of Finance. See http://www.joeran.de/dox/Bildungspaket_fuer_Sachsen-Anhalt.pdf.

11. See the Bitkom press release dated Nov. 9, 2016: "Eltern wünschen sich eine digitale Schule für ihre Kinder," https://www.bitkom.org/Presse/Presseinformation/Eltern-wuenschen-sich-eine-digitale-Schule-fuer-ihre-Kinder.html.

12. See http://www.de.digital/DIGITAL/Redaktion/DE/Digital-Gipfel/Video/2017/Digital-Gipfel-20170613/20170613-keynote.html.

13. Johanna Wanka, speaking at the Bitkom conference Bildung 4.0, Jan. 19, 2017, https://www.bmbf.de/de/bitkom-konferenz-bildung-4-0-3845.html. Given this tangled constellation of interests, it is no surprise that the authors of books supporting the digital revolution (e.g., Jörg Dräger and Ralph Müller-Eiselt, *Die digitale Bildungsrevolution: Der radikale Wandel des Lernens und wie wir ihn gestalten können* [Munich: Deutsche Verlags-Anstalt, 2015]) are often also members of the business-friendly Bertelsmann Foundation.

14. Wendy Brown, *Undoing the Demos: Neoliberalism's Stealth Revolution* (New York: Zone Books, 2015), 33. The central questions in teaching digital competence are thus: "What are the conditions for being able to successfully take part in the market? What is needed to act autonomously in a social and private environment?" (see the publicity statement for Werner Hartmann and Alois Hundertpfund, *Digitale Kompetenz: Was die Schule dazu beitragen kann* [Bern: hep Verlag, 2015]).

15. Sigmar Gabriel at the National IT Summit, Nov. 17, 2016, https://www.youtube.com/watch?v=WSMvpkOVjvU (at 7:10–8:30).

16. *Medienkompass 1* (Zürich: Interkantonale Lehrmittelzentrale, 2008), 24–25.

17. At the IT summit on Nov. 17, 2016, Merkel spoke about a time when "very many young teachers came and trained East German workers, giving them the needed qualifications." Merkel

added: "It's not simple because we're also conditioned to think that we get wiser as we get older. We also climb the ladder in our professions and don't expect to be confronted at the end of our working lives with everything we don't know." See https://www.youtube.com/watch?v=m_OkET8Ic8E, starting at 4:20. For the speech of the chairwoman of the Culture Ministers' Conference, see https://www.youtube.com/watch?v=MuE73DBgxYA&t=407s.

18. Colleagues of the German computer pioneer Konrad Zuse programmed the Zuse 22 to intone "Hänschen klein" as a joke. "Daisy Bell" (a song about being in love rather than setting out to discover the world) was the first song ever *sung* by a computer. The song features not only in *2001*, but also in the animated feature *Robots* (2005), in which the computer Bigweld sings "Daisy Bell" while it's being repaired. See Stefan Höltgen, "Zelluloidmaschinen. Computer im Film," in *Medienreflexion im Film: Ein Handbuch*, ed. Kay Kirchmann and Jens Ruchatz (Bielefeld: transcript, 2014), 293–316, at 302.

19. In "HAL," interestingly, it's the older detective who reacts to surveillance by artificial intelligence by saying: "That's the way it is." His younger colleague asks him, "You just accept that?"—to which he responds, "What am I supposed to do, throw away my mobile phone?"

20. Space does not permit a discussion of the fact that it takes more to teach a deeper ability to reflect on media than what teachers can learn from private research in the evening. It needs to become part of educators' formal training. For more on this topic, see "Digitale Immigranten" in my *Stumme Medien: Vom Verschwinden der Computer in Bildung und Gesellschaft* (Berlin: Matthes & Seitz, 2018), 134–153.

21. Such remote braking technologies are already being invented on the EU level. See https://www.telegraph.co.uk/news/worldnews/europe/eu/10605328/EU-has-secret-plan-for-police-to-remote-stop-cars.html. On the interest the police have in unpatched security gaps, see the program *Computer*

und Kommunikation of Sept. 16, 2017, on Deutschlandfunk Radio. On the use of facial expression and emotion recognition software in traffic situations, see the startup Eyeris in Palo Alto, California: http://www.eyeris.ai/.

22. See the Bayern 5 radio show, *Das Computermagazin*, July 23, 2017.

23. Ethik-Kommission Automatisiertes und vernetztes Fahren, June 2017 report, 20–21, 24, http://www.bmvi.de/Shared Docs/DE/Publikationen/DG/bericht-der-ethik-kommission .pdf?__blob=publicationFile.

24. Ethik-Kommission Automatisiertes, 23–24.

25. Pressemitteilung des Bundesministeriums für Verkehr und digitale Infrastruktur a,"Bundeskabinett verabschiedet Gesetzentwurf zum automatisierten Fahren," Jan. 25, 2017, http://www.bmvi.de/SharedDocs/DE/Pressemitteilungen/2017/011-dobrindt-gesetz-automatisiertes-fahren.html.

26. See Regula Stämpfli, "Lehrplan 21: Gesinnungssoldaten für Untertanenideologie," in *Einspruch! Kritische Gedanken zu Bologna, Harmos und Lehrplan 21*, ed. Alain Pichard and Beat Kissling (Uetendorf: self-published, 2016), 10 (helplessness); Markus Waldvogel, "Verordnete Unmündigkeit," in *Einspruch!*, 45 (warriors); Christoph Türcke, *Lehrerdämmerung: Was die neue Lernkultur in den Schulen anrichtet* (Munich: C. H. Beck, 2016), 18 (competence); Volker Bank, "Vom Wert der Bildung," in *Wozu Bildungsökonomie? Fachtagung des Deutschen Lehrerverbandes 2011* (Berlin: Deutscher Lehrerverband, 2012), 21–33 (autonomous capacity); Martha C. Nussbaum, *Not for Profit: Why Democracy Needs the Humanities* (Princeton, NJ: Princeton University Press, 2010), 2 (useful machines); Wendy Brown, *Undoing the Demos: Neoliberalism's Stealth Revolution* (New York: Zone Books, 2015), 188 (democratic citizenship).

27. http://www.cyberwise.org/what-is-digital-citizenship; see also https://www.youtube.com/watch?v=lKlJOxwyMWU.

28. See Brown, *Undoing the Demos*, 177; Mike Ribbles and Gerald Bailey, *Digital Citizenship in Schools* (Washington: International Society for Technology in Education, 2007), 2 (productive and responsible users). The didactic continuation of this approach is found at the *Ask a Tech Teacher* blog (https://askatechteacher.com) and the *Digital Citizenship Curriculum K-8* (Laguna Hills, CA: Structured Learning, 2013).

29. Charles Taylor, "Some Conditions of a Viable Democracy," *Eurozine*, Aug. 14, 2017, https://www.eurozine.com/some-conditions-of-a-viable-democracy.

30. On the German model of "constitutional patriotism," see the works of Jürgen Habermas. On the American variant, see Kwame Anthony Appiah, "Cosmopolitan Patriots," *Critical Inquiry* 23 (Spring 1997): 617–639.

31. Jon Katz, "Birth of a Digital Nation," *Wired*, April 5, 1997, https://archive.wired.com/wired/archive/5.04/netizen_pr.html.

32. Richard Barbrook and Andy Cameron, "The Californian Ideology," *Mute*, Sept. 1, 1995; quotes from the revised version of 2000: http://www.imaginaryfutures.net/2007/04/17/the-californian-ideology-2. On "reactionary modernism [as] economic progress and social immobility," see Barbrook, "Cyber-Communism: How the Americans Are Superseding Capitalism in Cyberspace," *Science as Culture* 9, no. 1 (1999): 5–40. I discuss the possibility of a digital nation beyond common values and divisive political standpoints in the chapter "Digital Nation" in my *Facebook Society* (New York: Columbia University Press, 2018).

33. John Erpenbeck and Werner Sauter, *Stoppt die Kompetenzkatastrophe! Wege in eine neue Bildungswelt* (Heidelberg: Springer, 2016), 26.

34. Cornelia Koppetsch, *Die Wiederkehr der Konformität: Streifzüge durch die gefährdete Mitte* (Frankfurt: Campus, 2013); Mark Lilla, "How Colleges Are Strangling Liberalism:

An Obsession with Identity Has Made Students Less Likely to Engage with a World beyond Themselves," *Chronicle of Higher Education*, Aug. 20, 2017, https://www.chronicle.com/article/How-Colleges-Are-Strangling/240909.

35. http://www.educationsymposium.net/archiv/2017/plenary program/.

36. *Medienbildung in der Schule, Beschluss der Kultusministerkonferenz vom 8 March 2012*, 3, http://www.kmk.org/filead min/Dateien/veroeffentlichungen_beschluesse/2012/2012 _03_08_Medienbildung.pdf. Karen Mossberger, Caroline J. Tolbert, and Ramona S. McNeal, in *Digital Citizenship: The Internet, Society, and Participation* (Cambridge, MA: MIT Press, 2008), include among "the aspects of participation in society online ... the impact of Internet use on the ability to participate as democratic citizens; and the effects of the Internet on the equality of opportunity in the marketplace" (2). For an early example of the philosophical-political approach, see Mark Poster, "Digital Networks and Citizenship," *PMLA* 117, no. 1, special issue: "Mobile Citizens, Media States" (Jan. 2002): 98–103.

CHAPTER 5

1. bell hooks, "Eating the Other: Desire and Resistance," in hooks, *Black Looks: Race and Representation* (Boston: South End Press, 1992), 21–39.

2. Lisa Nakamura, *Cybertypes: Race, Ethnicity, and Identity on the Internet* (London: Routledge, 2002).

3. In *Sand*, a stream of sand cascading down a video screen reacts to the projected silhouettes of observers.

4. Jameson, Frederic, *Signatures of the Visible* (New York: Routledge, 1992), 1.

5. Immanuel Kant, *Critique of Judgment*, paragraph 16.

6. Béla Balázs, *Der Geist des Films* (Frankfurt: Suhrkamp, 2001), 103; Rosalind E. Krauss, *The Originality of the Avant-Garde*

and Other Modernist Myths (Cambridge, MA: MIT Press, 1985), 210; Martin Seel, "Adornos Apologie des Kinos," in *Wieviel Spaß verträgt die Kultur? Adornos Begriff der Kulturindustrie und die gegenwärtige Spaßkultur*, ed. Günter Seubold and Patrick Baum (Bonn: DenkMal Verlag, 2004), 127–144, at 136.

CHAPTER 6

1. See European Commission, "Communication on a European Agenda for the Collaborative Economy," June 2, 2016, http://ec.europa.eu/DocsRoom/documents/16881. On "corporate nullification" see Frank Pasquale and Siva Vaidhyanathan, "Uber and the Lawlessness of 'Sharing Economy' Corporates," *Guardian*, July 28, 2015, https://www.theguardian.com/technology/2015/jul/28/uber-lawlessness-sharing-economy-corporates-airbnb-google.

2. Scott Simon, "Driver's Suicide Highlights 'Race to the Bottom' in Cab Industry, Union Director Says," NPR, Feb. 10, 2018, https://www.npr.org/2018/02/10/584757778/taxi-drivers-face-financial-crisis.

3. Noam Schreiber, "How Uber Uses Psychological Tricks to Push Its Drivers' Buttons," *New York Times*, April 2, 2017, https://www.nytimes.com/interactive/2017/04/02/technology/uber-drivers-psychological-tricks.html.

4. Clayton M. Christensen, *The Innovator's Dilemma: When New Technologies Cause Great Firms to Fail* (Boston: Harvard Business Review Press, 1997); for criticism of the inflationary use of the "disruptive innovation" and its application to Uber, see Clayton M. Christensen, Michael E. Raynor, and Rory McDonald, "What Is Disruptive Innovation?" *Harvard Business Review* (Dec. 2015), https://hbr.org/2015/12/what-is-disruptive-innovation)

5. Gary Hall, *The Uberfication of the University* (Minneapolis: University of Minnesota Press, 2016), xi; Trebor Scholz, *Uberworked and Underpaid: How Workers Are Disrupting the Digital Economy* (Cambridge: Polity, 2017), 8.

6. In 2014, Uber created, in various cities, maps of "RoGers": "anyone who took a ride between 10 p.m. and 4 a.m. on a Friday or Saturday night, and then took a second ride from within 1/10th of a mile of the previous nights' drop-off point 4–6 hours later," http://sanfrancisco.cbslocal.com/2014/11/18/uber-crunches-user-data-to-determine-where-the-most-one-night-stands-come-from.

7. Mike Isaac, "How Uber Deceives the Authorities Worldwide," *New York Times*, March 3, 2017, https://www.nytimes.com/2017/03/03/technology/uber-greyball-program-evade-authorities.html.

8. Tim O'Reilly, "Open Data and Algorithmic Regulation," in *Beyond Transparency: Open Data and the Future of Civic Innovation*, ed. Brett Goldstein and Lauren Dyson (San Francisco: Code for America Press, 2013), 289–300, at 293.

9. Victor Luckerson, "The Rise of the Like Economy," *The Ringer*, Feb. 15, 2017, https://www.theringer.com/2017/2/15/16038024/how-the-like-button-took-over-the-internet-ebe778be2459.

10. See Julia Carrie Wong, "Uber Concealed Massive Hack That Exposed Data of 57M Users and Drivers," *Guardian*, Nov. 22, 2017, https://www.theguardian.com/technology/2017/nov/21/uber-data-hack-cyber-attack.

CHAPTER 7

1. As of spring 2017, the video is no longer available at the original YouTube-Site but can be found at other sites under the title "Mercedes Benz Adolf Spot" or "Mercedes spot 2013 (unofficial)."

2. For the documentation of the results of the audience votes, see http://terror.theater/cont/results_main/en. It is hardly surprising that jurists have vehemently protested their disempowerment in favor of a legally entirely uninformed referendum, among them Wolfgang Schild, a professor of

criminal law who wrote a polemic, *Verwirrende Rechtsbeleh-rung: Zu F. von Schirachs "Terror"* (2016), and Federal Judge Thomas Fischer, who wrote on the subject in his column in the German weekly *Zeit* on May 17, 2016 (http://www.zeit.de/gesellschaft/zeitgeschehen/2016-05/literatur-strafrecht-fischer-im-recht) and on Oct. 18, 2016 (www.zeit.de/gesellschaft/zeitgeschehen/2016-10/ard-fernsehen-terror-ferdinand-von-schirach-fischer-im-recht/komplettansicht). On experimental ethics, see the anthology of essays *Experimental Ethics: Toward an Empirical Moral Philosophy*, ed. Christoph Lutge, Hannes Rusch, and Matthias Uhl (New York: Palgrave Macmillan, 2014).

3. Ethik-Kommission Automatisiertes und vernetztes Fahren, report, June 2017, 11, 18, https://www.bmvi.de/SharedDocs/DE/Publikationen/G/bericht-der-ethik-kommission.html?nn=12830.

4. See http://moralmachine.mit.edu; dilemma 6 of 13; https://www.nhtsa.gov/nhtsa/av/av-policy.html (26–27). See also *Autonomes Fahren: Technische, rechtliche und gesellschaftliche Aspekte*, ed. Markus Maurer, J. Christian Gerdes, Barbara Lenz, and Hermann Winner (Berlin: Springer, 2015); "Why Self-Driving Cars Must Be Programmed to Kill," *MIT Technology Review*, Oct. 22, 2015, https://www.technologyreview.com/s/542626/why-self-driving-cars-must-be-programmed-to-kill; Cory Doctorow, "The Problem with Self-Driving Cars: Who Controls the Code?," *Guardian*, Dec. 23, 2015, https://www.theguardian.com/technology/2015/dec/23/the-problem-with-self-driving-cars-who-controls-the-code; Cade Metz, "Self-Driving Cars Will Teach Themselves to Save Lives—but also Take Them," *Wired*, June 9, 2016, https://www.wired.com/2016/06/self-driving-cars-will-power-kill-wont-conscience.

5. Jean-François Bonnefon, Azim Shariff, and Iyad Rahwan: "Autonomous Vehicles Need Experimental Ethics: Are We Ready for Utilitarian Cars?" (published online, Oct. 13, 2015,

https://arxiv.org/pdf/1510.03346v1.pdf); "The Social Dilemma of Autonomous Vehicles," *Science* 352, no. 6293 (2016): 1573–1576. Bonnefon, Shariff, and Rahwan also developed the concept for MIT's Moral Machine. For Senior Manager Active Safety Christoph von Hugo's statement on Mercedes-Benz's safety-and-sacrifice strategy, see https://blog.caranddriver.com/self-driving-mercedes-will-prioritize-occupant-safety-over-pedestrians. We of course assume that this Mercedes rule would not apply in that variant of MIT's Moral Machine where the choice is between the death of a dog as the sole occupant of the vehicle (and why wouldn't you let Fido drive off by himself to go and stay with your parents?) and the demise of a female bystander.

6. Ethik-Kommission, Automatisiertes und vernetztes Fahren, 19, n. 3.

7. Ethik-Kommission, Automatisiertes und vernetztes Fahren, 16.

8. In the case of the trolley problem, the cultural difference expresses itself, for instance in the fact that far more Americans than Chinese would be prepared to switch the tracks or push the fat man from the bridge. The reason may be the emphasis of Taoism and Buddhism on nonintervention or in the authoritarian system of government in China, which doesn't encourage individuals to take responsibility for making decisions. See Henrik Ahlenius and Torbjörn Tännsjö, "Chinese and Westerners Respond Differently to the Trolley Dilemmas," *Journal of Cognition and Culture* 12, nos. 3–4 (2012): 195–201. It is also interesting in this context that the majority of the performances of Schirach's drama in China and Japan (3 of 5 in Beijing, 12 of 19 in Tokyo, 3 of 4 in Nishinomiya/Hyogo) are among the few that ended with a guilty verdict (162 of 1747 worldwide as of May 22, 2018) (http://terror.theater/cont/results_detail/de).

9. Simon Parkin, "Teaching Robots Right from Wrong," *Economist*, June–July 2017; Franco Moretti, *Distant Reading* (Konstanz: Konstanz University Press, 2016).

10. Max Eyth, *Poesie und Technik*, quoted in Ernst Cassirer, "Form und Technik," in Cassirer, *Symbol, Technik, Sprache: Aufsätze aus den Jahren 1927–1933*, ed. Ernst Wolfgang Ort and John Michael Krois (Hamburg: Meiner, 1985), 39–91, at 74.

11. Johann Gottfried Herder, "Über die Wirkung der Dichtkunst auf die Sitten der Völker in alten und neuen Zeiten" [On the effect of poetic art on the ethics of peoples in ancient and modern Times], in *Herders Sämmtliche Werke* (Berlin: Duncker & Humblot, 1969), vol. 8, 339; Martin Heidegger, *Off the Beaten Track*, ed. and trans. Julian Young and Kenneth Haynes (Cambridge: Cambridge University Press, 2002), 232.

12. John von Neumann, *Theory of Self-Reproducing Automata*, ed. Arthur W. Burks (Champaign: University of Illinois Press, 1966); "Our AI systems must do what we want them to do": "An Open Letter: "Research Priorities for Robust and Beneficial Artificial Intelligence," Jan. 2015, http://futureoflife.org/ai-open-letter.

13. Jussi Parikka, *The Anthrobscene* (Minneapolis: University of Minnesota Press, 2014). On an "exit" from this period of the Anthropocene, see Bernard Stiegler, *Automatic Society: The Future of Work*, vol. 1 (New York: Wiley, 2017); on a world without humans, see Ludueña Romandini, *Para além do princípio antrópico: Por uma filosofia do outside* (Buenos Aires: Cultura e Barbárie, 2012).

14. Richard H. Thaler and Cass R. Sunstein, *Nudge: Improving Decisions about Health, Wealth, and Happiness* (New Haven, CT: Yale University Press, 2008); Sarah Conly, *Against Autonomy: Justifying Coercive Paternalism* (New York: Cambridge University Press, 2013).

15. Dieter Mersch, *Ordo ab chao—Order from Noise* (Zurich: Diaphanes, 2013), 18.

16. Cassirer, *Symbol, Technik, Sprache*, 316.

17. Yvonne Hofstetter, *Das Ende der Demokratie: Wie die künstliche Intelligenz die Politik übernimmt und uns entmündigt* [The end of democracy: How artificial intelligence is taking over politics and disenfranchising us] (Munich: C. Bertelsmann, 2016).

18. Nick Bostrom, *Superintelligence: Paths, Dangers, Strategies* (Oxford: Oxford University Press, 2014); cf. chapter 12: "Acquiring Values," 226–255.